RANTERS, REVIVALISTS AND REFORMERS

Hull University Press

Monographs in Regional and Local History

No. 2

Cover Hugh Bourne (Source: Methodist Archives and Research Centre, John Rylands University Library of Manchester MAM PLP 10.44.1.); William Clowes (Source: BBC Hulton Picture Library).

RANTERS, REVIVALISTS AND REFORMERS:
PRIMITIVE METHODISM AND RURAL SOCIETY
SOUTH LINCOLNSHIRE 1817-1875

R. W. AMBLER

Senior Lecturer in History
School of Adult and Continuing Education
University of Hull

HULL UNIVERSITY PRESS

1989

© R. W. Ambler 1989

British Library Cataloguing in Publication Data

Ambler, R. W.
  Ranters, revivalists and reformers:
  Primitive Methodism and rural society, South Lincolnshire
  1817-1875.
  1. Great Britain. Society. Role of Methodist churches, history
  I. Title   II. Series
  261.1'0941

ISBN 0-85958-480-1
ISSN 0951-8916

Phototypeset in 11 on 12pt Times and printed by the Central Print
Unit, the University of Hull, and bound by Khromatec Ltd.

Contents

Acknowledgements

This publication is one product of a long period of work on the social and religious history of Lincolnshire and during that time I have incurred a large number of debts. Professor John Saville of the University of Hull provided help, stimulus and encouragement during the time when the Ph.D. thesis on which this study is based was being prepared. In this context I am also grateful to Professor N. McCord, Dr R. J. Olney and Mr D. M. Woodward. My discussions with Dr James Obelkevich at an early stage of the work were of great benefit.

I also wish to acknowledge assistance from the staff of the Lincolnshire Archives Office; the Methodist Archives and Research Centre, first at City Road, London, and then at the John Rylands University Library of Manchester; the Public Record Office; the Brynmor Jones Library, the University of Hull; the British Library Newspaper Library at Colindale; the former Hartley Victoria College; the Revd Dr E. W. Baker, Secretary of the Methodist Conference for permission to consult Primitive Methodist Conference journals when they were in his custody; the ministers of Boston, Holbeach, Sleaford and Spalding Methodist circuits and Mr R. Warnes of Messrs Godson, solicitors, Sleaford for access to material; Mr M. W. L. Brown of Quarrington, the Lincolnshire Standard Group of Newspapers, the East Midland Allied Press and the staff of Grantham Town Library for allowing me to work on their collections of newspapers; Mr D. Wattam of Grimsby Central Library, Humberside Libraries and Arts.

Thanks are also due to Mr G. Burrows, Mr M. J. Elsden and Mr N. Leveritt of the Spalding Gentlemen's Society; and also to the President and Council of the Society who gave permission to use the photographs of Holbeach, Pinchbeck West and Spalding Primitive Methodist chapels as illustrations, while the Revd Peter W. Robinson located the picture showing Gosberton Clough Primitive Methodist chapel owned by Miss C. M. Leverton. Other illustrations of chapels are from the collection of negatives belonging to the Lincolnshire Methodist History Society and made by the Revd William Leary. I am grateful to Mr J. S. English for arranging the use of these as well as to Miss Alison Peacock,

Methodist Church Archivist, for assistance with illustrative material in her care. Mr J. Spencer of the Photographic Service of the University of Hull helped to prepare the illustrations while Mr K. Scurr drew the maps. An earlier version of some of the material on fenland chapels appeared as a paper in volume 23 of the series of Studies in Church History - *Voluntary Religion* - and I am grateful to the Ecclesiastical Society for permission to use it in this study.

Mrs J. Cook prepared the typescript for publication and I would also like to thank Dr J. M. Bellamy and Miss J. M. Smith of Hull University Press for their help and advice.

Behind these considerable debts there lies the support of my wife and family to whom I make the customary, but none the less heartfelt acknowledgement for their help in the continuing and absorbing task of attempting to understand something of the lives of the people of Lincolnshire in the past. The responsibility for errors, omissions and shortcomings is mine.

Grimsby   R.W. Ambler
May 1989

List of Figures and Illustrations

Figures

Illustrations

Abbreviations

A.H.R.	*Agricultural History Review*
B.G.	*Boston Guardian and Lincolnshire Advertiser*
D.S.N.	*Drakard's Stamford News*
E.L.	*English Labourer*
G.J.	*Grantham Journal and Lincolnshire, Leicestershire and Nottinghamshire Advertiser*
J.R.A.S.E.	*Journal of the Royal Agricultural Society of England*
L.	*Labourer*
L.A.O.	Lincolnshire Archives Office
L.R.S.M.	*Lincoln, Rutland and Stamford Mercury*
L.U.C.	*Labourers' Union Chronicle*
P.M.Mag.	*Primitive Methodist Magazine*
P.P.	Parliamentary Papers
P.R.O.	Public Record Office
s	Shilling(s)
S.F.P.	*Spalding Free Press and Eastern Counties Advertiser*
S.G.S.	Spalding Gentlemen's Society

Glossary

Camp Meeting   Open air gathering for preaching and prayer which usually lasted for a whole day. In North America, where they originated, camp meetings might stretch over several days.

Circuit   The Primitive Methodists adopted the Wesleyan Methodist system of organisation by which local groups of members, or **societies**, were arranged in **circuits**. The circuit was the basis on which services in the chapels and meeting places of the area were arranged and local affairs were managed. Both full-time and part-time preachers went from place to place according to a **plan** of services while the circuit was governed by a **quarterly meeting**.

Class   The society in each place was grouped into **classes**, the membership of which was renewed quarterly by a minister.

Local Preacher   Local preachers were laymen who, while still pursuing their secular occupations, preached and conducted services in their spare time. They were usually not paid for this, but some local preachers were paid to work full-time and were designated **hired local preachers**.

Mission   The word **mission** is frequently used as a verb by Methodist writers to describe the process of establishing a mission or presence in a place. For this sense see *Collins Dictionary of the English Language* (1979 ed.). The term **mission** is also used as a noun to refer to an embryonic circuit without full independence from the parent circuit out of which it had developed.

Plan	See **Circuit.**
Quarterly Meeting	See **Circuit.**
Society	See **Circuit.**
Travelling Preacher	The term **travelling preacher** was used to describe full-time, paid Primitive Methodist ministers.
Trustee	The ownership of chapels was vested in **trustees** who acted on behalf of the connexion and were responsible for the maintenance and upkeep of the buildings.

Introduction

In his monumental study *The Origin and History of the Primitive Methodist Connexion* published about 1905, H.B. Kendall skilfully portrays the rich diversity of Primitive Methodism's development in the nineteenth century.[1] He resurrects the now lost chapels and meeting places of the period, peopling them with the ordinary men and women who were the mainstay of their support. The book's many illustrations give a firm sense of place to the spiritual and institutional development of the Primitive Methodist connexion which Kendall chronicles. His achievement is all the more remarkable because his analysis is built up from a sound understanding of the significance of the local communities in which the Primitive Methodists lived and worshipped.

One strong impression that comes from looking at the many photographs which Kendall reproduces is that Primitive Methodism was a working-class church.[2] Yet this generalisation conceals considerable diversity in the connexion's development which can be best understood — as Kendall himself demonstrates — in terms of the local communities in which the Primitive Methodists took root. The fact that Primitive Methodism flourished in the mining areas of the north-east as well as in the agricultural villages of East Anglia or the fishing communities of the Yorkshire coast demonstrates its capacity to minister to the spiritual needs of different types of community. At a more local level the reasons for its success or failure in neighbouring places adds a further dimension to any analysis of the connexion's development.

This study is concerned with the development of Primitive Methodism in the southern part of the county of Lincolnshire from its arrival in the area in 1817 to 1875. By the last date the onset of agricultural depression and depopulation were affecting the nature of the rural society in which Primitive Methodism had taken root. The beginnings of the agricultural trade union movement in the 1870s also raises questions about the extent to which the Primitives made a distinctive contribution to its development. This in its turn provides useful indications of the nature of the connexion's relationship with rural workers.

1

2

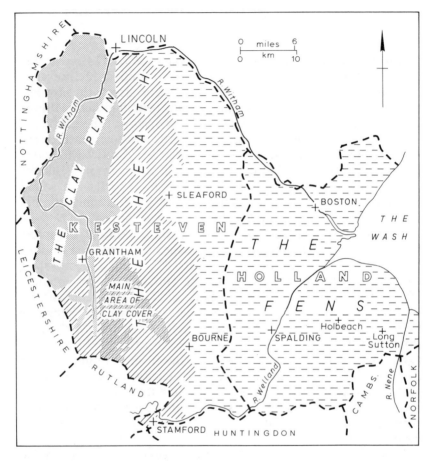

Fig.1 South Lincolnshire main topographical features.

The southern half of the county of Lincolnshire — formerly the ancient Holland and Kesteven divisions of the county — although predominantly agricultural, is of interest because of its considerable diversity. It was also relatively small — about forty miles from Lincoln in the north to Stamford in the south and about the same distance from the shores of the Wash to the borders of Nottinghamshire on the west and south-west. The main geographical districts within it were the fenlands to the east, the limestone heath in the central part and the clay valley of the River Trent to the west. The local communities reflected the characteristics of the area in their varied social composition. The large and scattered communities of freeholders, small farmers and the tradesmen and craftsmen who served them were a distinctive feature of the fenland district. Closely controlled estate villages were more significant on the part of the heath where many of the landed gentry of the area had their residences. Yet these local variations in settlement patterns did not exclude more subtle differences and contrasts. Villages with contrasting social structures could be found next to each other, while others were of a more mixed character with some of the features of both types of village. For example, on the edge of the fens, where the uplands of the Lincolnshire Heath were joined by the low-lying fenland on the east, the large freeholders' village of Metheringham had as its much smaller neighbour the estate village of Blankney. Scopwick, to the south of Blankney, while having land belonging to the Blankney estate, and being much influenced by it, also had some of the characteristics of a freeholders' community.

The whole of south Lincolnshire experienced considerable economic and social changes in the course of the nineteenth century. The effects of these differed from area to area, from community to community and indeed within the social groups which made up local society. This meant that the sixty-year period of this study, when the Primitive Methodists established themselves in south Lincolnshire, was one in which the lives of the people were changed in many ways depending on a number of inter-related factors: where they lived, what they did for a living, their age and family circumstances. The ways in which Primitive Methodism interacted with these different social conditions is the basis of this local study.

Any success which Primitive Methodism achieved was based on

its ability to provide a religious experience which was appropriate to the needs of people caught up in this web of change. It offered new opportunities and ultimately a new sense of security, using a meaningful framework of language and imagery with which it conveyed its message. In its early Ranter phase Primitive Methodist preachers were carried forward on a wave of revivalistic ardour, exciting opposition among those to whom its enthusiasm seemed to err dangerously near to a degree of excess which might threaten the existing religious and ultimately social order.

Mere enthusiasm was not enough, however, to sustain it. While some converts might find their way into other churches there were others who had come out of them, seeking the stronger revivalistic fare which gave the Primitives their particular identity. Before they reached Lincolnshire they had already created an organisation out of the various strands of revivalism which had united to form the embryonic Primitive Methodist connexion.[3] This provided the means whereby full-time preachers were to be paid and the expanding work of the Primitive Methodists sustained and developed. If more souls were to be saved new converts needed to add their support — pecuniary as well as moral — to the movement. Preoccupations needed to be shifted towards the maintenance of institutions as well as the salvation of individuals.

The mental processes and spiritual yearnings of individual converts might not impinge to any great extent on the communities where they lived and worked, beyond worrying those who cared, that a propensity to hurry after strange itinerating preaching outsiders might be indicative of a desire to subvert existing institutions. However, when these began to take the more concrete forms of regularly organised cottage meetings and then of chapel buildings, the reality of Primitive Methodism could not be ignored.

Chapels not only needed financial support to build and maintain them, but also land on which they could be built. It was at this point that differences between the development of Primitive Methodism in various types of village communities began to become apparent. Where landlord control prevented chapel building the growth of Primitive Methodism was stunted, so that by the middle of the nineteenth century it had become associated largely with the freeholders' villages where land could be obtained. The fervour of the early Ranter preachers had carried them into a wide range of communities, but local conditions were an important factor which influenced the places where they were able to put down their roots and develop into a settled denomination.

These freeholders' communities gave more than the liberty to buy and sell property. They also allowed a degree of autonomy in the way a person could behave. This might be less attractive to the casually employed agricultural labourer earning his or her living by the day than to the village tradesman, craftsman or small farmer who might amass enough capital to invest in the local property market. None the less, despite the considerable limitations of economic circumstances, one of the options available to the inhabitants of the freeholders' villages was religious choice. Moreover, for those who felt comfortable in the atmosphere of the Primitive Methodist chapel, where working-class leaders and members played a significant part, they could exercise this freedom at a number of levels. Full commitment after initial conversion, leading to attendance not only at Sunday worship but also at week-night activities as well as an involvement in local chapel affairs through service as a lay officer or preacher, represented one end of a spectrum. The other might be only occasional attendance at annual events such as Sunday school anniversaries in support of children who were themselves brought under Primitive Methodist influence by their weekly attendance at the school.

Other choices open to people living in the pluralistic society of the freeholders' villages of south Lincolnshire in the nineteenth century might include friendly societies, the public house or beershop, or a mixture of these. Villagers could be eclectic even contradictory in their attitudes, so it would be a mistake to look for total consistency in the way in which they shaped their lives. Occasional attendance at the Primitive Methodist chapel, where the virtues of teetotalism were preached, would not necessarily rule out visits to the beerhouse. Similarly, the desire to make some financial provision against possible misfortune through a friendly society might, paradoxically, bring an individual into the ambit of the local public house where the society held its meetings. The atmosphere here contrasted with the attitudes which the developing national friendly society movement sought to inculcate among its members with its emphasis on the cultivation of the virtues of thrift and self-help.

Some people showed greater outward consistency in their attitudes and conduct. Chapel members, who were assiduous in their attendance at both Sunday and week-night services, meetings and functions as well as being committed to the temperance ethic, which was early and enthusiastically endorsed by the Primitive Methodists, would find that these provided a full round of social activity. The disciplinary machinery of the connexion ensured that they would not stray into those organisations which might endanger its reputation or their own souls. Moreover, the fact that Primitive Methodism was able to offer the opportunity for members to develop a way of life based on the local chapel and its activities also brought them into the ambit of reforming organisations concerned with wider issues than individual salvation. Having acquired a social base in the chapel they were able to participate in the causes and movements over which the Nonconformists, including the Primitive Methodists, increasingly began to share a common platform. Issues such as disestablishment, education and teetotalism often first became prominent in south Lincolnshire in the towns. These were then taken up in the villages of the area. In this the circuit organisation of the Methodists was an effective medium of communication and was copied by other bodies.

The building of chapels and the need to maintain them as well as to uphold the connexion to which they belonged meant that there was a constant need to ensure that they were supplied with monetary as well as moral support. In order to attract as many people as possible to chapel activities there was increasing emphasis on their entertainment element. This did not mean that the tone of these activities compromised the wholesome ethic of chapel life and they retained a distinctive tone which separated them from the drink-based culture of the public house. Moreover, the concern to save souls which had first brought the Primitive Methodists into south Lincolnshire still remained even if to some extent it became subsumed in the need to maintain institutions.

Revivalism was a continuing element in Primitive Methodist life, even if on a different basis to that of the early open air Ranter preachers. Revivals continued to be looked and prayed for even if they were to take place inside chapel buildings and, like the open air camp meetings (see Glossary) which had now become an annual event, more a matter of routine than the result of the charismatic movement of the spirit.

Souls were still sought, but once they had been saved they could join the ranks of those who strengthened the institutions of the connexion. Revivalism sustained existing structures and ceased to be the free-flowing spiritual force which had carried the Primitive Methodists out of the confines of Wesleyan Methodism in the early years of the nineteenth century. It also became increasingly inward-looking as the need to bring into membership children and grandchildren of the early converts, together with the rising generations of Sunday scholars, became apparent.

The problems of maintaining the institutions of religious life were not exclusive to the Primitives. The other branches of Methodism, as well as the Baptists and Congregationalists, where they existed in south Lincolnshire, also needed to uphold buildings, pay ministers and maintain worship. These obligations were met in similar ways so the forms of Nonconformist social and religious life came increasingly to resemble each other in the course of the nineteenth century. The unity engendered by a common approach to such issues as education and temperance also tended to subsume any particular characteristics of the individual denominations in pursuit of common goals. In the case of the Primitive Methodists this was a further stage in their integration into a common Nonconformist culture which minimised any tendency they might have possessed to create what has been referred to as a distinctive and characteristically Primitive Methodist 'religious counter-culture'.[4]

In all of this the Primitive Methodists were carrying forward their working-class membership. It was the place of this membership in the 'Revolt of the Field' of the 1870s that provides the basis for an analysis of the extent to which the Primitives of south Lincolnshire had developed into a 'labour sect'.[5] Primitive Methodists can be enumerated as among the most active members of the agricultural trade union movement, but it is important not to treat them in isolation from the other religious and reformist movements in south Lincolnshire of which they were one. It has already been noted how the pluralism of life in the freeholders' villages of the area provided opportunities for the inhabitants of south Lincolnshire to build up ways of life which did not necessarily mean that they were totally committed to one particular organisation or movement. The agricultural trade union movement emerged from this background so that its early members found their inspiration from a number of sources. While the Primitive Methodism of the national leader Joseph Arch undoubtedly helped to shape his attitudes, assumptions and rhetoric, other union leaders like William Banks, the Boston republican stationer, worked within another ideological framework. The differing emphases which these men brought would appeal to the varied strands in the lives of the agricultural labourers of south Lincolnshire so that aspects of one part of the trade union movement would appeal more to some than to others. As in other movements which were important in village life in the second half of the nineteenth century, ideas and leadership also came out of the towns adding a further element of variety to its development. Since Primitive Methodism made no corporate response to the agricultural trade union movement, but sought to adopt a neutral position, its influence was reduced. When this neutrality led to the use of chapels being forbidden for union meetings it could even be interpreted as hostility.

The way in which Primitive Methodism came to assume a more central place in village society can be seen not only in the documentary evidence but also in the architecture of the chapels and meeting-houses illustrated in this book (see Centre-fold). From the unpretentious chapel at Gosberton Clough, which served the needs of an isolated fenland community, the modest architectural development which took place shows an increasing consciousness of appearance and style. The town chapels at Boston, Holbeach and Spalding represent its culmination in this period. These three buildings also demonstrate the increased importance of the towns of the area in local Primitive Methodist life in the second half of the nineteenth century, while their relatively greater architectural pretensions reflect the concern of their builders to maintain an appearance worthy of a church which had moved towards the centre of local Nonconformist life.

These illustrations can only provide an indication of the appearance of the many chapels that have now gone from the Lincolnshire countryside. In the twentieth century buildings have disappeared as a result of declining Methodist membership and the amalgamation of village societies which followed the union of the various branches of Methodism in 1932. This means that there are few tangible reminders of the significant contribution which

Primitive Methodism made to the life of the area. None the less, as this study seeks to show, the importance of the Primitive Methodists was their ability to work within a particular set of social circumstances, creating new opportunities for their followers based on a distinctive type of religious experience.

I

South Lincolnshire 1817-1875

The first Primitive Methodist preachers to enter south Lincolnshire came into an area which was undergoing considerable social and economic change. The effect of this on the lives of the people was an important element in creating the mental climate within which Primitive Methodism took hold and developed. One measure of this change was the rapid growth of population in the first half of the nineteenth century which more than doubled from 89,959 in 1801 to a peak of 185,357 in 1851, excluding the city of Lincoln. The most rapid period of growth was between 1801 and 1821, but from 1851 to 1871 it began to drop declining by just over 1 per cent.[1] The growth was almost entirely due to natural increase and not migration into the area. In 1841 nearly 90 per cent of the people of south Lincolnshire had been born in the county.[2] There was also considerable outward migration which was greater among women than men, so that the ratio of men to women differed markedly from that of the country as a whole until 1871, while these differences were even more pronounced in the case of people under twenty.[3]

The slight drop in the total population of the area between 1851 and 1871 was associated with decreases in the number of people living in many villages and changes in their occupations. Agricultural work, which was the most important activity in south Lincolnshire throughout the period, became relatively less significant by 1871 as the numbers employed in farming declined.[4] The three largest towns in south Lincolnshire — Boston, Grantham and Lincoln — all developed as industrial centres and grew rapidly down to 1871. Like the smaller towns of Bourne, Holbeach, Sleaford, Stamford and Spalding, some of which also had a small amount of manufacturing activity, they continued to act as marketing and service centres. The village of Long Sutton also developed as a market and as a result of the growth of the Wash port of Sutton Bridge.[5]

There were also changes in rural trades and crafts in the area in the second half of the nineteenth century. Work which had previously been carried out by village craftsmen was increasingly performed in towns, while the number of tradesmen grew as their businesses spread into the country towns and villages and the traditional means of retail distribution such as the market and fair, were replaced by shops and similar settled outlets.[6] The rate at which women migrated out of the county reflected the limited employment opportunities for them in south Lincolnshire, the largest number of jobs being in domestic service and in work based on sewing and clothing. Just over 2000 adult women were employed in sewing in south Lincolnshire in 1861 while there were nearly 5000 adult female domestic servants.[7] The amount of farm work carried out by women varied from area to area and was seasonal.[8]

These changes in the size and composition of the population were associated with a period of considerable agricultural development which had begun in the late eighteenth century. The effect on the landscape, social relationships and way of life of the people varied between the three main geographical areas of south Lincolnshire — the fens to the east, the heath between them and the western clay plain which stretched to the River Trent in the west. (See Fig. 1) In physical terms the changes were more dramatic in some parts than in others, but none was untouched by them. By the middle of the nineteenth century the geological and geomorphological variations had begun to have a less marked effect on agriculture than they had in 1815. Yet these differences were not entirely eliminated and the effect of agricultural change on them was an important factor in the development of the area.[9]

The landscape and economy of the fens was transformed by drainage and enclosure at the end of the eighteenth and beginning of the nineteenth centuries. Before drainage, large areas of the low lands were subject to inundation by water and their economy was based on pastoral husbandry: the rearing of beasts, sheep and horses; the sale of fish, fowl, hemp and flax.[10] After drainage and enclosure this was replaced by an economy based on arable husbandry which increased in efficiency as drainage was improved further in the course of the nineteenth century. The exploitation of the rich natural resources of the fens before drainage provided the basis for an independent life-style which, according to Arthur Young, produced 'a mischievous race of people'.[11] The new style of fen farming was epitomized by Matthew Allen of Brothertoft who:

before the enclosure and draining of Holland Fen, paid 20*s*. rent for a cottage and croft. His stock on the fens was 400 sheep, 500 geese, seven milch cows, ten or twelve young horses, and ten young beasts . . . He now rents about 50 acres of the enclosure at 25*s*. an acre; has a wife, five children, and two servants, and greatly prefers his present situation, not only for comfort, but profit also.[12]

Sheep and cattle continued to be important in the fens even after the expansion of arable farming so that the agriculture of the area was diversified. Moreover, since the richness of the soil meant that the fen farmer was not restricted to one course of husbandry he could also adapt the pattern of his cropping to meet changing circumstances. As communications improved with the coming of the railways the range of crops increased further to include vegetables and soft fruit for sale in the large towns.[13]

Like the fens, parts of the limestone mass of the Lincolnshire heath also underwent considerable change in the late eighteenth and nineteenth centuries. In its northern part the limestone did not provide rich natural resources. This meant that before enclosure in the late eighteenth and early nineteenth centuries the area was given over to extensive sheep walks on which the small 'heath' sheep could find a living while other parts had come to be used as rabbit warrens.[14] After enclosure the limestone heath was brought into cultivation but needed good management based on a rotation of turnips, barley, artificial grasses and wheat together with generous applications of manures to prevent it reverting to gorse and warren.[15] Once the heathland farmer had embarked on a course of high farming he could not change dramatically in the face of price fluctuations.[16] Philip Pusey's description of the heath between Lincoln and Sleaford in November 1842 provides a vivid picture of the transformation which had been effected on the limestone soils. The area presented:

a cultivated exuberance such as I had never seen before. . . for miles we passed on through fields of turnips without a blank or a weed, on which thousands after thousands of long-woolled sheep were feeding in netted folds; and so large as well as regular were the turnips in the narrow rows, that the lower halves which remained in the ground, when the upper half had been consumed, seemed to pave these sheep-folds.

Every stubble-field was clean and bright; all the hedges kept low, and
neatly trimmed; every farm-house well-built, with spacious courts,
and surrounded by such rows of high, long saddle-backed ricks, as
showed that the land did not forget to return in August what it had
received from the fold in December . . .[17]

The southern heath is largely covered with chalky boulder clay
with only a very narrow band of limestone left uncovered. Its
landscape of broken relief, small hedged fields and winding roads
contrasted with the newly-enclosed limestone heath and the fens.
In the nineteenth century the district was more remarkable for its
woods, parks and game preserves than for the excellence of its
farming.[18] The area had been enclosed early and there was a high
proportion of grassland, so that arable farming was subsidiary to
the breeding and fattening of cattle. However, the proportion of
arable increased during the nineteenth century so that by 1875 the
southern heath had become an area of mixed farming.[19]

Like the southern heath the pace of agricultural change on the
low clay plain to the west of the limestone upland was less
dramatic than in the fens or on the limestone. Two-thirds of the
area was under grass at the beginning of the nineteenth century.
Sheep and cattle were bred and fattened with some being brought
in from the heath. The needs of the graziers had led to early
enclosure, but where the clay lands were covered with gravel to the
west and the south-west of Lincoln nearly a quarter of the land
survived as open moorland and meadow into the period of
parliamentary enclosure. In spite of the preponderance of
grassland the arable farming of the area, although technically
backward, did produce cash crops such as wheat and barley as well
as supplying fodder for its livestock.[20] The few remaining open
field parishes which were left in the area were enclosed in the
second half of the eighteenth century, but this was not necessarily
a prelude to the improvement of arable farming. Old habits
lingered on, while the lack of under-drainage until after 1831
reduced the quality of cereal crops and made sheep vulnerable to
disease. As the century progressed there was, however, a
continuous increase in the amount of arable land in the area so
that, as in the other pastoral areas of Lincolnshire, the old style
grazier of the end of the eighteenth century who had little arable
land, was replaced by a new style of mixed farmer.[21]

The differences between the fens, the heath and the western
valley of south Lincolnshire began to break down as new

agricultural techniques made farmers less dependent on the inherent characteristics of the land they farmed.[22] By 1825 the amount of arable land in the area had been increased by the conversion of the fens and the heath to tillage, while further increases were to come from ploughing up permanent grassland. In spite of price fluctuations this process went on continuously from the 1820s so that by 1875 the pattern of agricultural activity throughout south Lincolnshire was much more uniform than it had been at the beginning of the century.[23]

Changes in the agricultural economy of the area were associated with social change. In the fens the replacement of the old economy and way of life evoked popular opposition in the form of a communal football match which was held over disputed lands in Holland Fen in 1768. The use of this traditional vehicle of protest emphasised the deep-rooted nature of the change and opposition to it.[24] There is no evidence of similar direct opposition to enclosure and the cultivation of the limestone heath, although the changes which took place were equally fundamental. Since it lacked the natural riches of the fens and only gave a limited yield from traditional agricultural techniques, the occupiers of this part of the heath did not constitute a well-defined interest which was disturbed by change. After enclosure the area developed a distinctive economy with a labour force provided by at least part of the increased population of the area.[25]

The disappearance of the old style grazier on the early enclosed areas of the heath and the western lowlands also brought changes in outlook, even if they were less sudden than in other areas. The decline of the independent interest in politics was one indication of this since the grazier, with his lower level of rent and labour bill compared with the arable farmer, had different priorities in the disposition of his wealth and the pursuit of his livelihood.[26]

The large number of common rights which existed in the fens before drainage and enclosure were carried over to create a distinctive social structure in the area. In this, property in every parish was divided among many owners. Several leading landowners who lived in the Kesteven division had estates in the fens of Holland and there were also a few large corporate landowners, but the resident squire was almost entirely absent. At the beginning of the nineteenth century Gosberton, for example, had a huncred and sixty landowners and Quadring over a hundred and fifty.[27] A considerable proportion of these owners farmed their own land, although numbers might vary from parish to parish, but, whether farmed by its owner or not, the small farm was a significant part of the fenland economy and this was a continuing and distinctive characteristic of the area throughout the nineteenth century.[28] The fens were not, however, entirely devoid of large farms and when the opportunity had presented itself after drainage some of Lincolnshire's largest holdings had been established there.[29]

If the large numbers of small farms were the distinguishing characteristic of the fenlands of south Lincolnshire, the estates of resident landed gentry were a marked feature of the heath. It contained some of the largest farms in south Lincolnshire, especially to the north of Sleaford and to the south of Grantham and these large farming units made possible the considerable capital investment and management economies which were necessary to bring the limestone uplands under cultivation.[30] The tenant farmer continued to be the main type of occupier of these farms to the 1870s and beyond, while their ownership remained with the same landed families.[31]

The farms on the western lowlands were predominantly small although, as in the other areas of south Lincolnshire, there were considerable differences in their size so that there was also a greater proportion of large farmers than in any other part of the area except the heath. The landed estates of the Thorolds of Syston, Sir Robert Heron of Stubton and George Hussey Packe of Caythorpe were an important influence in the southern part of the area between Grantham and Newark. However, in a number of parishes over a fifth of the farmland was occupied by owners and the small farmer was particularly important in the area to the west and south-west of Lincoln. Here parishes with a predominance of small farms lay next to those with a few large holdings and while a few parishes had a considerable number of owner-occupiers, others were in the sole ownership of a squire.[32]

* * * * * *

As a result of agricultural change the various areas of south Lincolnshire developed distinctive settlement patterns which were still marked in the 1870s although all areas were affected to some degree by settlement dispersal as farms, public houses, the lodges of estates, windmills and the buildings associated with railways were developed away from village centres.[33] The heath and the fens were largely devoid of habitation outside the villages before enclosure and drainage, but, with the dispersal of settlement which followed these, their differing structure of landownership and size of farms meant that they developed different settlement patterns.[34]

As new houses and barns were built at the centre of the new farm units on the limestone heath fear of creating poor law settlements led to a restriction in the number of cottages which were built.[35] The resulting settlement pattern of the area was described by Edward Stanhope in 1867:

> The Heath district between Lincoln and Sleaford, comprises a large tract of land recently brought into cultivation, and belonging to a few large landowners, such as Mr. Chaplin, Lord Bristol, and Mr. Nisbit Hamilton. Two lines of villages, from five to seven miles apart, form its eastern and western boundaries, and between them there is not only an absence of villages, but almost of cottages also. Brauncewell, for instance, comprises 3,470 acres, divided into three farms, all the property of Lord Bristol. For the supply of labour to these parishes there are only 13 cottages (five of them with one bedroom only). Ashby-de-la-Lund [*sic*] Bloxholm, and Temple Bruer are not better supplied, while the tract north of these villages is almost entirely without cottages. The main feature therefore of this district is that the labourers are all congregated into the larger towns.[36]

A similar pattern developed on the limestone heath to the south of Grantham, but in those parts covered by boulder clay secondary settlements had grown up in the large parishes of the area during the Middle Ages, while the landed estates had been an influence on the landscape from before the beginning of the nineteenth century.[37] Its 'large trees of beech, lime, ash, &c.' made the clay-covered area of the heath an attractive place for landed gentlemen to live and pursue their leisure activities.[38]

There was considerable movement of population into the fens at the beginning of the nineteenth century. Settlement spread along the new roads and drains while the dispersal of population was increased by the high proportion of farmers who moved out to live on the large number of smallholdings in the area.[39] When larger farm units had been created, they were also built away from the older centres of population in the middle of their fields. However, not enough cottages were built for the workers on them and, although the number gradually increased, the supply did not begin to catch up with their needs until the end of the nineteenth century.[40]

Where parliamentary enclosure took place in the western lowlands of south Lincolnshire it led to a similar pattern of settlement dispersal to that in other parts of south Lincolnshire, also affected by parliamentary enclosure. In the parish of Doddington, for example, neither the farms on the Moor, nor those known as Top House, the Grange, the Birk Springs, the Carr Lane, nor the Carr Farm had homesteads built on them in 1749, but by 1778 they all had houses.[41]

*   *   *   *   *   *

The social life of the villages of south Lincolnshire evolved in response to the pattern of landownership and agricultural development in the areas where they were situated. Contemporary writers placed villages on a spectrum of types of village community stretching from the 'closed' or 'close' village at one end to the 'open' village at the other. The closed village was one in which the ownership of land and house accommodation was in the hands of one, or at most three, proprietors who shared similar interests and where the owners had the power, whether or not they shared the inclination, to control settlement within it. In an 'open' parish it was not possible, because of divided ownership, to exercise a similar degree of control.[42] Ashby de la Launde, with its resident squire who owned all the parish and was also vicar and patron of the living, represented the extreme type of closed village. Leake, in the fens north-east of Boston where the soil belonged to 'many freeholders' was an open village at the opposite end of the spectrum of village types. In between were closed villages such as Digby or Cranwell, where the owner did not actually reside, or Howell, which although closed, had three proprietors, but where one was resident at the Hall and so able to exercise a degree of control over the life of the local community. Beyond this point divided landownership meant that the influence of landlords was less strong and villages such as North Witham, with three owners (one being an institution) and none resident, could be described as open.[43]

Nearly 62 per cent of the 237 settlements in south Lincolnshire were open and their distribution was related to the varied patterns of local landownership. The predominance of freeholders in the fens meant that the villages of the area were open. This was not only in the heart of the fens but also many of the places which lay along the eastern slope of the heath, where parish boundaries stretched across a number of different types of land from the heath in the west to the fens in the east. Similarly, the majority of villages on the western escarpment of the heath overlooking the western lowlands of south Lincolnshire were also open, except to the immediate north and south of Grantham, where the estate villages of Syston, Belton, Little Ponton, Stoke Rochford and Harlaxton were situated. Here the estates of the landed gentry were of greater importance than in other parts of south Lincolnshire, as they were on the heath where there was also a number of closed villages. In the western lowlands a mixture of settlement types prevailed with a cluster of open villages around Foston, Long Bennington, Hougham, Westborough, Dry Doddington and Claypole; North and South Hykeham, together with Thorpe on the Hill, Swinderby and North Scarle and Bassingham, and Carlton le Moorland a few miles to the east were also open villages. This situation remained fundamentally unchanged through to the 1870s.

The differences between open and closed villages were seen not only in their landownership but also in their social and economic life.[44] The absence of landlord control of settlement meant that the open villages were not only larger but that their size reflected the movement of the population of the area as a whole. In the closed village on the other hand population levels were less predictable. The closed village of Bloxholm had a population of 81 in 1801. Its highest level was 116 in 1811 and its lowest 67 in 1841. These somewhat irregular figures fluctuating around a comparatively low initial level contrasted with those for the nearby open village of Ruskington which had a population of 483 in 1801. This rose each decade until 1871 when it reached 1156. The open fenland community of Leake had 911 people in 1801, reached its height in 1851 with 2062, fell to 1912 in 1861 and then rose again to 1952 in 1871.[45]

In the closed village, with the squire at the apex of its hierarchical social structure, the parson and the tenants of the largest farms beneath him, going down to the labourers at its base, the social composition of the community was less varied than in an open village.[46] At Bloxholm in 1856 the squire, rector and four farmers were the dominant element in the village's social life out of its total population of 105.[47] The control exercised by the landlord of the closed village over the behaviour of its inhabitants distinguished it from its open neighbours. Arthur Young described the labourers living on the estate of the Duke of Ancaster in south Lincolnshire as 'remarkable for being orderly, decent, church-going men, who behave themselves well'.[48] By carefully vetting the character of all tenants, whether they were farmers, labourers or craftsmen, a landlord could attempt to ensure that they would behave in an acceptable way. If they did not he had the ultimate sanction of eviction.

As well as conferring privileges the ownership of a village also brought obligations, the fulfilment of which both enhanced the status of the donor while confirming the subservient position of the recipients. The provision of housing on a landed estate enabled a landed gentleman to regulate the lives of his tenants while at the same time, by building model dwellings, often suitably ornamented, he added to the visual impact of the property. This can be seen in an account of Earl Brownlow's village of Londonthorpe, near Grantham, which he rebuilt in 1849.[49] The writer was:

> at once struck with the neatness of its newly erected, and as we supposed, *model* cottages and gardens, with a wash-house in common on the opposite side of the road, containing a mangle and 'other appurtenances thereto belonging', not omitting to mention a useful as well as ornamental looking pump placed under cover at the entrance and for the joint use of the fortunate tenants. There has evidently been great pains bestowed upon making matters comfortable in this village. It must be solid gratification to the landowner to know that his humble cottagers are contented and grateful, while his more

> wealthy tenants admire him for the amount of happiness
> which he dispenses about them. . .[50]

If the owner of a village lived at a distance his ties to it could be weakened. A correspondent from Sleaford, where the absentee Marquis of Bristol owned large amounts of land, signing himself as 'An old Tenant who has never seen his landlord' noted that the Marquis had only paid one visit lasting not more than a few hours to the area from which he drew many hundreds of pounds in rent. The Marquis who, it was said, knew no more than half a dozen people personally on this part of his estate, was contrasted with the other large proprietors of the neighbourhood who were 'Ever easy of access, kind and courteous on all occasions, *presiding at their own audits*, &c., they are fully acquainted with the feelings and requirements of those who have the happiness to live under them, and are looked up to as the friend and benefactor of all.'[51]

Paternalism and the deferential behaviour which was associated with it extended beyond the confines of the relatively limited number of strictly closed villages with resident squires. Lord Brownlow's influence, for example, went beyond his Kesteven estates to include his property in the fenland. In 1816 he was in correspondence with his agent about the distribution of Bibles and Prayer Books to the poor of Gosberton and the maintenance of the village's church school. He was also involved in the distribution of flour, wheat and coals to the poor of Pinchbeck.[52] An appeal to Lord Willoughby measured the possible extent of his patronage in the village of Aslackby, where he had 1150 out of 3800 acres against the amount of land he owned there when he was asked in 1847 to contribute a quarter of the salary of a parish schoolmaster.[53]

Open villages lacked the clear sense of authority which a controlling landlord or landlords provided. The Revd Samuel Hopkinson, writing in about 1825, described how the lack of a landlord's influence affected behaviour in the open village of Morton near Bourne:

> let the magistrates be ever so active, let the resident clergy be
> ever so attentive, while the property of this large parish
> continues divided and in so many hands, each individual

proprietor will consider himself at liberty to act independently. His example is insensibly imitated by his inferiors who gradually growing up in . . . lawless habits, have no notion of that decent deportment and necessary subordination visible in market towns and villages belong[ing] solely either to some virtuous nobleman, or to a resident gentleman.[54]

The lack of any strong source of authority meant that open villages could become centres of criminal activity where there was some tolerance of such crimes as poaching, incendiarism, the theft of food and animal maiming among a working population who were not as well insulated from hardship as people who lived in communities protected by a degree of paternalism. In this respect alone the difference between the lives of people in open and closed villages can be illustrated from the arrangements which were made in 1831 to pay the labourers on the Ancaster estate at Grimsthorpe to watch for poachers with the gamekeeper. This effort to preserve game would divide these men from their counterparts in the open villages, creating fundamentally different patterns of behaviour as a result of the varied social conditions in which they lived.[55]

As new demands were made upon the labour force by the development of agriculture in south Lincolnshire the differences between the open and closed villages were exacerbated. A distinction developed between the regular labour force, who were given preference by landlords in the provision of housing, and the floating reservoir of labour which was employed at busy times of the year, but laid off when work was slack. Houses were provided in the closed villages for the regular workers on the farms and the estate, together with some for former regular workers who had become old or unfit, or for their widows. In newly-cultivated areas under the control of landed estates restrictions on settlement were enforced tightly and the amount of accommodation for the workforce was strictly limited. The regular work on the new farms was carried out by unmarried men, hired on a yearly basis, who lived as farm servants in the farm house or were boarded with one of the married farm workers who lived nearby. These married men lived in the limited amount of cottage accommodation which was provided on the farm. In this way the farmers' needs for foremen, shepherds, stockmen, wagoners and horsemen were supplied, while the custom of hiring farm servants for a limited period avoided the creation of a poor law settlement.[56]

The less regular and seasonal labour on these farms was provided by men who lived in the open villages and walked out each day to work where and when they were needed. Women and children were also part of this labour force until their employment was regulated in the 1860s and 1870s.[57] In some areas they had been organised in gangs since the 1820s but by 1867 children were often employed in preference to women because they were cheaper and available for work earlier in the morning.[58]

The open villages also became the centres in which those trades and craftsmen who provided their services to their local community and the area around it lived, together with some professional men such as surgeons, druggists and veterinary surgeons. Some craftsmen went from farm to farm to do their work while others established workshops in a village where work was brought to them. Similarly pedlars and travelling salesmen took their wares out into neighbouring villages, while village shopkeepers were dependent on customers coming in to them. In the large fenland parishes some of the trades and craftsmen lived in the outlying settlements which had grown up away from the villages. While some trades and craftsmen worked on their own, others might have larger establishments and employ either apprentices or hire journeymen who had finished their training.[59]

*   *   *   *   *   *

A variety of ways of life grew out of the different social and occupational patterns which developed in south Lincolnshire in the nineteenth century. An individual's place within these depended on whether he or she lived in an open or a closed village, what were their means of livelihood and by whom they were employed. Their position also changed as they found work, left their parental home, married, settled in a particular place and had children. In the closed villages the deferential behaviour expected of their inhabitants gave little scope for the development of a lifestyle which did not conform to that expected by their proprietors; and, as long as the structure of landed estates in south Lincolnshire remained intact, this was unlikely to change. The ways of life and attitudes of the people of the open villages did however change within the relative freedom which these communities afforded.

Contemporary commentators noted how the quality of the relationship between farmers and their employees was altering in the course of the nineteenth century so that a lack of sympathy appeared to be developing between them. This meant that 'the labourer has no longer his employer's interest at heart; he becomes an eye-servant; his conduct is regulated by the opinions of his own class'.[60] The Lincolnshire agricultural writer John Algernon Clarke noted in 1852 how labourers had been 'driven by proprietors unwilling to augment the poor's-rate, to crowded freehold villages many miles from the place of their labour'.[61] It was said that in these 'neglected' open villages:

> Many of the men get irregular and uncertain work. Their employers take little or no interest in them or their families. The men themselves have no feeling for the place and are ready to leave it any day; they are always in an unsettled state, living from hand to mouth . . . The clergyman of the parish has little chance of getting at them.[62]

Farm workers who lived with their employers on annual hirings were also affected by changes in their relationships with farmers. One indication of this was the trend which was thought to exist towards boarding these farm servants outside the farmers' own houses. This was apparent in the parish of Heckington in the second half of the nineteenth century where they lived with ground-keepers who acted as resident farm foremen or managers.[63]

The ties between master and man also became less rooted in custom and practice and increasingly based on cash payment. Richard Healey, a farmer from Laughton near Folkingham pointed out in 1827 how farmers were becoming more like manufacturers so that it was impossible for them to pay what might be described as a 'fair' price for their labour irrespective of the level of their profits.[64] What was seen as a more rational work discipline emerged, unencumbered by inefficient custom and practice so that, for example, the introduction of the mechanical reaper was seen as having moral force as well as bringing economic advantages. It enabled 'the time honoured custom' of supplying food and drink in the harvest field to be commuted to cash payments, so ending the situation in which the farmhouse kitchen became 'a place very much akin to the taproom of a public house' and drunkenness and accidents were a common occurrence in the harvest field.[65]

Comments on the changing relationship between farmers and their workmen need to be set against the background of the wide range of farm sizes in Lincolnshire. These went from the small unit which only employed one man to those with a labour force of over sixty and the relationship between master and man would differ across this range.[66] There was no marked change in the overall balance of farm sizes in south Lincolnshire after 1815, apart from a slight increase in the importance of the larger farm.[67] The distribution of the various sized farms and their differing workforces was to some extent determined by geography, but there was always a sufficient mix of farms to prevent the labourers who worked on one from becoming rigidly separated from those who worked on another.

The quality of the relationship between farmers and their workers was determined by the extent to which the farmers were able to influence the behaviour of their men outside working hours. This in turn depended on where a man actually lived — whether in the centre of a village or outside it in a cottage on the farm where he worked, as well as whether the village in which he lived was open or closed. As the basis of the relationship between the farmer and his workers was reduced to the purely contractual the leisure and recreational activities of the labourers ceased to be an area over which the employer had any influence, particularly in the open villages. Harwood Mackinder, who had a large farm at Halton Holegate in north Lincolnshire, said in the 1860s that he could not play any significant part in the lives of those of his labourers who lived away from his farm: 'Where my labourers live now, neither my wife nor I can take any real interest in them or their families; put them on my farm and we shall feel it our duty to look after them and do what we can for them.'[68]

This change in the relationship between masters and men left an increasing area in the lives of the farm workers in which they were free to develop their own ways of life. This growing independence was reflected in reports of the behaviour of farm servants during their leisure time at Hough on the Hill in 1860s. Here 'the youths in the employment of farmers and some idle lads' created scenes of 'riot, insult and disorder' around the church porch and yard on Sundays when their conduct was 'unnoticed by masters and churchwardens'.[69] In the late 1860s Mr Charles North who farmed 1400 acres at South Thoresby in north Lincolnshire said that the labourers were no longer prepared to stand 'like beasts to be sold' at annual hiring fairs, but that they had begun 'to enquire about their masters' character' and to 'combine a little for some purpose'.[70]

Women and children involved in field work also evolved a way of life which rejected the values of polite culture and Victorian ideals of feminine conduct. This was especially true of those who lived in the open villages which were the centres for this type of employment.[71] Girls of sixteen years of age and over were said in 1843 to prefer field work to domestic service because of the freedom it gave them in the evenings and on Sundays.[72] Children involved in field work attended school irregularly and left at an early age. This gave them the freedom to develop their own way of life and a spirit of 'independence' not imposed from above by the educational system.[73] The Revd Henry Leigh Bennett, curate of Long Sutton, referred to the 'immense difficulties' he faced in the 1860s and felt that it was hardly possible to inculcate 'any real moral or religious training or habits of obedience'.[74]

This independent spirit began to develop in the second half of the nineteenth century into a greater willingness to become organised in pursuit of improved working conditions. Men working at a threshing machine at the Black Swan inn at Spalding went on strike in 1855 following the refusal of beer at '"'lowance"' hour and only resumed after it has been supplied.[75] In 1857 men inthe Lincoln area were well enough organised to meet the farmers in a body 'like cool, practical men' to discuss wage rates, while by 1866 the labourers employed on a farm at Wrangle Common had reached the stage of striking for a wage increase.[76] Where the relationship between farmers and labourers was still touched by paternalistic attitudes and assumptions these might still be employed by the redress of grievances. During the harvest of 1849 English reapers in many places combined to raise wages but those in the Blankney area sought the mediation of Charles Chaplin, the local landed magnate.[77]

Like the agricultural labourers, the tradesmen and craftsmen who lived in the open villages developed different attitudes and ways of life in the course of the nineteenth century from those living the the closed villages of south Lincolnshire. A master tradesman or craftsman in an open village might build up surplus capital which could be invested in either a house or land, while also having some degree of influence over his smaller customers who might be indebted to him. On the other hand, if his business was on a small scale he might be vulnerable to the influence of his more powerful customers such as gentry, clergy and farmers.[78] In a closed village his position would be similar to that of the 'regular servants' of the landed estate who received 'the good treatment normal of their class'.[79]

The position of a tradesman or craftsman, who was an employee rather than a master, or of an apprentice, was more akin to that of an agricultural labourer. These men first began to organise themselves in the market towns of the area and by 1872 town-based trades unions played an influential role in the early development of the agricultural workers' union.[80] Unlike the more substantial farmers the master tradesmen and craftsmen, with their smaller households, were less distant from those of their employees who lived with them. The important positive influence a master could exert on the life of a young apprentice was emphasised in Methodist biographies such as that of Thomas Fawcett of Sleaford who was converted during his apprenticeship.[81]

* * * * * *

In his account of the village of Scopwick in the 1830s its vicar, George Oliver, described the three phases in the life of the agricultural labourers. After the age of fourteen, when they were judged 'capable of following the plough' they left irregular field work and became annually-hired farm servants, while they 'quit their desultory servitude' on marriage and endeavoured to find work as 'confined labourers'.[82] This account is deficient in not providing an account of the irregularly employed day labourers who did not enjoy the 'certain work' of the inhabitants of closed villages or of the yearly hired or confined farm workers. It does, however, illustrate the extent to which individuals changed roles as they took up the various employment opportunities which opened up to them during their working lives — changes which also involved moving from place to place to find employment.[83] The lives of agricultural workers in south Lincolnshire during the nineteenth century were therefore built-up out of a series of experiences resulting from a complex inter-relationship between where they lived, where they worked and the work which their job required. These experiences were in their turn lived out against the background of considerable economic and social change and development shared by all social groups living in the area. New horizons and the opportunity to create and develop new ways of life, which also extended to religious experience, emerged particularly in the open villages. It was in this *milieu* that Primitive Methodism took root and developed.

II

Early Primitive Methodism and its Movement into Lincolnshire

Primitive Methodism had its origins among a number of revivalist groups on the fringes of mainstream Wesleyan Methodism at the beginning of the nineteenth century. Its founding fathers Hugh Bourne and William Clowes shared the evangelical fervour and taste for unconventional spirituality of these people and their experiments with a wide range of religious experience carried them out of the confines of Wesleyan Methodist discipline which sought to channel their activities into a pattern of orderly spiritual development. The strength of the revivalists lay in their ability to reach beyond existing denominational structures and offer a dynamic religious ethos which reflected the tensions of the everyday lives of people caught up in social change. The conservative position of the Wesleyan Methodist leadership might commend itself to the governing classes, but it also emphasised the potential for division within Methodism between those whose interests lay in stability and those for whom the ebb and flow of revivalism was a reflection of the instability of their own position in society. What distinguished the Primitive Methodists was the way in which the revivalistic energies which took them out of the constraints imposed by official Wesleyan Methodist policy were brought together in a connexional form, giving scope for lay participation in church government. Groups such as the Band Room Methodists of Manchester, the Independent Methodists of Macclesfield, the Quaker Methodists of Warrington and the Magic Methodists of Delamere Forest developed a local base and made moves towards some form of union of their various branches. The Primitives were however able to move beyond this, uniting the driving force of American Methodist frontier-style revivalism with the visions and prophetic insights, as well as Quaker-style spirituality, which these local groups had cultivated, and to expand beyond their local base in the Burslem area of Staffordshire to become a national church maintaining a separate existence until Methodist Union in 1932.[1]

The American revivalist, Lorenzo Dow, who was visiting England between December 1805 and April 1807 made contact with, and helped to link, the groups which had developed both within and on the periphery of Wesleyan Methodism, particularly in Lancashire and Cheshire.[2] Hugh Bourne first met Dow towards the end of his visit in April 1807 when, during a visit to Harriseahead on the edge of the Potteries, he heard him preach and describe American camp meetings (see Glossary). Dow also visited Burslem, Tunstall and Congleton, where William Clowes, as well as Hugh Bourne's brother, James, also heard him. The Bournes were strongly influenced by Dow's experience as well as the accounts of camp meetings which had appeared in the *Wesleyan Methodist Magazine* between 1802 and 1806 and they decided to attempt to introduce them into Staffordshire.[3] The first they arranged was held at Mow Cop, a Pennine crag on the border between Staffordshire and Cheshire, on 31 May 1807. William Clowes was present together with people from Burslem, Congleton, Knutsford, Macclesfield, Warrington and other places where Dow had preached and where revivalists were active.[4]

Further similar meetings were held and in June 1808 Hugh Bourne was expelled from the Wesleyan Methodist connexion under the terms of a decision made at the 1807 national conference to condemn and disclaim all connection with camp meetings.[5] Thomas Cotton, one of his associates, was expelled shortly afterwards.[6] William Clowes, however, remained a Wesleyan Methodist member until September 1810, although his name had been removed earlier from the preachers' plan (see Glossary) for attending camp meetings.[7]

These meetings provided a focus for revivalist activities, but they had no well-defined organisational base. While on the one hand they attracted support from groups of people associated with the revivalist sects outside mainstream Methodism, on the other many of the new converts who were made at them joined the Wesleyan Methodists.[8] This continued even after Hugh and James Bourne hired James Crawfoot as a full-time preacher and paid him from their own pockets.[9] However, by 1810 the need to provide a more structured oversight for this activity was becoming apparent and, according to Hugh Bourne, it was felt that 'from providential circumstances as well as Divine impression' it appeared to be 'the will of God that we as a Camp Meeting community should form

classes and take upon us the care of Churches'.[10] Preachers
organised by Hugh Bourne and his associates were visiting thirteen
places on a regular basis by July 1810 as well as conducting
missionary work and holding camp meetings.[11] During the second
half of 1810 Bourne was evangelising in Staffordshire, Cheshire
and Lancashire as well as extending his activities into Derbyshire.
In the early autumn of 1810 he visited London accompanied by
James Crawfoot. It was during this visit that they called on Joanna
Southcott and, although Bourne concluded that she was 'in
witchcraft' their contact with her is an indication of the extent to
which they were prepared to seek spiritual experiences on the
fringes of conventional Christian piety.[12]

After his expulsion from the Wesleyan Methodists, William
Clowes gathered a small group of followers round him and also
began to undertake preaching tours including a visit to Derbyshire
with Hugh Bourne and James Crawfoot. In December 1810 during
a depression in the potting industry he began to work full time as a
preacher supported by the contributions of some of his religious
associates.[13] In May 1811 the revivalist groups associated with
Hugh Bourne came together with Clowes's followers — an
amalgamation which took place against a background of tension,
accompanied by expulsion from the local Wesleyan Methodists
which helped to sharpen the development of the new
organisation.[14] Membership tickets were issued, following
Wesleyan Methodist practice, to the members of the new
organisation so that what had been hitherto various groups of
people supporting revivalist activity began to evolve into a more
disciplined body. The issue of tickets regularised the contact
between members and the preachers who visited them while
providing the opportunity to organise financial support for the
work, although this was initially still on a voluntary basis.[15] The
building of a chapel at Tunstall in Staffordshire in 1811 was a
further significant step in the development of a permanent
organisation and in June 1811 a preaching plan was issued showing
fifteen full and part-time preachers serving eight places. The
adoption of the title 'Primitive Methodist' in February 1812
marked the development of a separate identity for the new body
from out of the sectarian groups where it had originated.[16] Many
of the characteristics of these groups were carried over into the
new Primitive Methodist connexion, including fervent prayer

meetings held under shared leadership, open air preaching and large-scale participation in worship, as well as personal evangelisation through conversation.[17]

Tunstall was the only circuit (see Glossary) in the Primitive Methodist connexion until 1816 when one was formed based on Derby. This was superseded by Nottingham circuit in 1817 and from 1818 to 1819 there were three — Tunstall, Nottingham and Loughborough.[18] The period immediately following 1811 was not however marked by any great geographical or numerical advances and was to some extent a period of consolidation, including the preparation of a set of rules for the connexion.[19] In the Primitive Methodist heartland of the Potteries there was a strong impetus to consolidate existing work based on a sound organisation and a diligent pastorate working through established societies rather than to expand through evangelical enterprise.[20] The differences between the expansionists and the consolidators have been seen as a continuation of a distinction between the group of people who were associated with Hugh Bourne and the followers of William Clowes, but a further potential cause of difference was between those who had come into Primitive Methodism after expulsion from the Wesleyan Methodists and converts from the outside. Some of the former Wesleyans were said to be 'popular and more talented than the rustic Primitives' so that they were allowed to preach at greater length at camp meetings although their style was described as more suitable 'for the sanctuary, and not for the field pulpit'.[21]

In spite of the Tunstall circuit authorities' wish not to enlarge the connexion's base their position was undermined by the activities of the preachers and the build up, which had begun in 1810, of Primitive Methodism in the villages of south-central Derbyshire was continued.[22] William Clowes took part in this expansion into Derbyshire and by 1817 and 1818 he had crossed into Nottinghamshire and Leicestershire.[23] These hesitant advances into the east Midlands were caught up in the great Midlands revival of religion of 1817 to 1818.[24] Its progress was described by George Herod who was a contemporary witness of the events of the period:

> In about one year and nine months not less than seventy-five towns and villages were missioned (see Glossary) and had

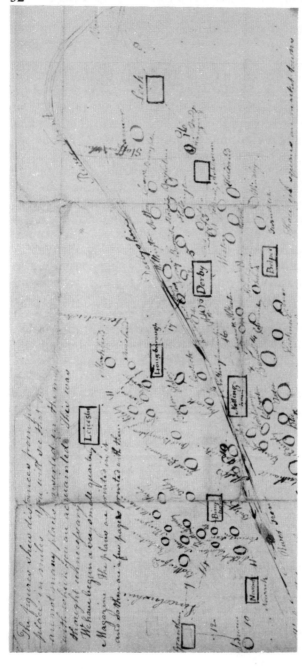

Fig.2 Sketch Map showing the eastward expansion of Primitive Methodism, 1818. The top of the map is orientated south. The River Trent is shown running from the top right to the bottom left with Grantham and Leadenham ('Lednam') in Lincolnshire to the extreme left. Towns are indicated by a square with the distance in miles given between places. The purpose of the map was to give 'an idea of the enlargement of the work of God among us'. (Source: Methodist Archives and Research Centre, John Rylands University of Manchester MAW MS. 73.4.4.)

regular worship established at them on Lord's days; and not less than seventy-five local preachers and exhorters were raised up and had their talents brought into operation, in supplying appointments, and aiding and holding Camp-Meetings.[25]

The revival partly coincided with Lorenzo Dow's third and final visit to Britain in 1818-19 when he made contact with the Primitive Methodists and, according to his own account, visited between thirty and forty chapels in Derbyshire, Leicestershire and Nottinghamshire.[26] As well as helping to stimulate or promote revivalistic activities Dow may also have helped to reconcile some of the tensions within the connexion.[27] His style of American revivalism provided a way forward for the Primitives as they sought to reconcile the need to come to terms with the evangelistic freedom, which had alienated their early followers from Wesleyan Methodism, with the build up of the necessary institutional framework to support their work.[28]

These activities reached to the borders of Lincolnshire by 1818 when Dow opened a Primitive Methodist chapel at Bingham just over the county boundary in Nottinghamshire. The new building was said to be 'not sufficient to hold half the people assembled' so that in the afternoon Dow and a female Quaker preacher 'addressed the multitude in the market place'.[29] Dow had begun the open air service by singing one of his American hymns 'which the people had been accustomed to sing for some months past' and 'hundreds joined in the grand chorus of hallelujah!'[30] People had travelled from a wide distance to hear Dow preach and his success, together with the fact that it was possible to open a chapel in the area, can be attributed to the work of William Clowes and John Wedgwood who had evangelised on the Lincolnshire-Nottinghamshire border in 1817.[31]

Wedgwood was a former potter of private means who, until he became a paid travelling preacher (see Glossary) in 1829, worked unpaid for the Primitives. His presence on the frontiers of the connexion's missionary activity is an indication of the extent to which its work was still relatively uncoordinated since the free-lance status of such preachers as Wedgwood meant that they were far less amenable to central control than men or women paid from Primitive Methodist funds.[32] Clowes and Wedgwood met at

Newark, where they both preached, and later at Grantham, following Wedgwood's imprisonment after he had attempted to conduct a meeting from the steps of the town's market cross.[33] Clowes's contact with Wedgwood also meant that he saw the results of the work of another unpaid revivalist, John Benton, whose activities also illustrate the loose way in which early Primitive Methodism moved forward. Benton 'paid very little attention to forming classes (see Glossary), and introducing rule and order; — his sphere was to break up the fallow ground, by entering into new places, preaching the truths of the Gospel, and converting sinners from the error of their ways.'[34]

Clowes gave a vivid impression of the heady atmosphere of this revivalistic work and of the prospects which seemed to be opening up for the Primitive Methodists as they expanded eastwards out of Nottinghamshire in a letter he wrote to Hugh Bourne. This was sent after a camp meeting at Skillington on the Lincolnshire border when he wrote: 'Such a field for labour I never saw. All around the country — east, west, north and south, they were crying, Come and help us!'[35] Clowes's presence in 1817 and also in 1818 may represent an attempt to bring some sort of order into the evangelistic work which was being carried on in the area, but even in his case it is difficult to construct a precise chronology of his movements at this period.[36] As the early Primitive Methodist preachers, some of whom were official travelling preachers and some of whom were freelance, moved the connexion onwards it became the task of its leaders and organisers to pull their work together. They 'gathered the converts into classes, appointed leaders, and made arrangements for local preachers (see Glossary) to supply newly-opened places'.[37] Even so, in many cases there was not a smooth transition from evangelisation to organisation and, what might often appear to be the first visit of preachers to a place was, in fact, the first which was recorded in diaries or memoirs. For example, the travelling preacher Francis Birch visited one of the Suttons in the south Lincolnshire fens in September 1820, but there had apparently been preaching there previously. Only the memory that eggs had been thrown at the preacher remained.[38] John Hallsworth found when he preached at Lincoln in 1820 that some of the people he had converted more than two years earlier while 'wandering up and down in this part of the country, sowing the word of God' were 'blessed, for they had heard the word of God and kept it'.[39]

In December 1818 William Braithwaite and Thomas Saxton, two preachers from the Nottingham circuit, entered the town of Gainsborough. Their activities, as described by Thomas Cooper, show the impression made by Primitive Methodist preachers at this time:

> One Sunday morning, I ran out, with a crowd of the neighbours, to hear two men who were singing aloud as they walked along the street, in their way to the market-place, — 'Turn to the Lord and seek salvation!' They were called 'Ranters', by the crowd; but I soon learned that they termed themselves 'Primitive Methodists'. These men remained in the town for some weeks, and preached in the open air, and held meetings in houses; and the crowd, young and old, were greatly affected. Soon a society was formed, and they began regularly to preach in the very small chapel which John Wesley himself caused to be built, . . . but which had been occupied as a warehouse for some time . . .
>
> Many loudly earnest preachers came and preached in the little chapel; and prayer-meetings were prolonged till midnight, often. And many up-grown sinners professed to find the pardon of their sins. The change of heart and life was real in some. I remember well an elderly man, an inveterate cock fighter, being humbled and becoming a true penitent. This man lived, for many years afterwards, a consistent Christian life. Nor was his case a solitary one. On the other hand, there were some fearful backslidings.[40]

Braithwaite and Saxton moved out from Gainsborough into north-west Lincolnshire so that by 1819 about thirty places had regular preaching by the Primitives and chapels had been built at Scotter, Owston Ferry and Kirton in Lindsey.[41] As well as making converts from outside the existing churches, the Primitive Methodists were also at this stage gathering in people for whom the Wesleyan Methodists were not providing the revivalistic fervour which they sought. Samuel Sharp, a thatcher from the village of Messingham had been a Wesleyan. However, after a lapse of three years he joined the Primitives in 1819 together with 'some of the elders among the Wesleyans who had seen Primitive Methodism in the days of Wesley' and 'knew it again when they

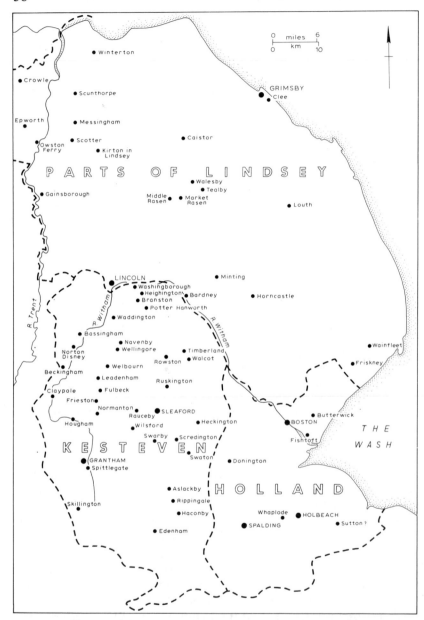

Fig.3 Centres of early Primitive Methodist activity in Lincolnshire mentioned in the text.

saw it in the days of Clowes and Bourne' so that 'a few among them ceased to be called Wesleyan and became Primitive.'[42] W. G. Bellham, a young Wesleyan Methodist local preacher and class leader, who lived in Gainsborough, heard a Primitive Methodist preacher for the first time in 1820. After a period of mental struggle he resigned his Wesleyan membership and offices, joined the Primitives and in 1821 began to work as a travelling preacher in the Scotter circuit.[43] However, although the work of William Braithwaite and Thomas Saxton resulted in the establishment of Primitive Methodism in an area which was later to be divided into nine circuits — Scotter, Gainsborough, Swinefleet, Goole, Selby, Epworth, Winterton, Crowle and Scunthorpe — Braithwaite's attitudes and approach to his work as a Primitive Methodist preacher had much in common with the early free-lance preachers who were linked to the connexion by sentiment and not by formal appointment as travelling preachers. Like them he appears to have had the private means which enabled him to follow an idiosyncratic course in his relations with the connexion and his strength lay in his ability to open up new places for them.[44]

John Oxtoby, another free-lance preacher, was a former East Riding agricultural labourer who supported his full-time evangelistic work from his savings. He had preached in 1818 in a number of villages in the Grimsby and Louth area with George Nicholson, a Wesleyan local preacher, and it was in the course of this work that he might have first heard of the Primitive Methodists.[45] Oxtoby was among the first to welcome William Clowes to Hull in January 1819. Here the Primitives were able to build their work on a revivalist tradition which reached back to the 1790s. The links which the Primitive Methodists had with the work of earlier revivalists was illustrated by the way in which Oxtoby joined Clowes in preaching expeditions to villages in the Hull area where Oxtoby had preached recently.[46]

In March 1819 John Harrison was appointed by the Primitive Methodist connexion to join William Clowes at Hull and the two of them crossed the Humber and began work in north Lincolnshire.[47] Harrison made further preaching expeditions in the area. In 1819 he came into contact with Sarah Healand who had gone with Ann Carr, 'a talented preacheress and great revivalist', from Hull in 1818 to preach at Market and Middle Rasen, Tealby, Walesby and Caistor.[48] The fact that he was in touch with Sarah Healand is a further indication of the contacts which early Primitive Methodist preachers had on the fringes of Wesleyan Methodist orthodoxy and with revivalistic activity outside the structures of the main religious bodies. Ann Carr, with whom she worked, had led classes for the Grimsby Wesleyan Methodist circuit in the Market Rasen area from where she came. Carr began to receive numerous requests to speak at services and meetings and even after the Wesleyans issued a ban on women preachers she continued to be active. She finally left them in 1814 when the creation of a new circuit based on Market Rasen led to a tightening of connexional discipline in the area and, after a period of free-lance activity, became associated with the group of 'preaching and praying women' with Wesleyan Methodist associations working in Hull and Nottingham. They contacted the Nottingham Primitive Methodist circuit quarterly meeting in December 1818 to request that a travelling preacher be sent to Hull.[49] Some of the tensions between the Wesleyans and the Primitives with their revivalist associates are evident in Harrison's account of a visit he paid with Sarah Healand to the house of a Methodist local preacher in Caistor. In spite of the fact that the preacher had invited them to call, he received them 'with indifference' and treated them disrespectfully. According to Harrison's account:

> He told us we were come to make a division. I informed him he was under a mistake, for we wanted none of his sheep, but those that were upon the mountains, which had no shepherd; — we did not come to call the righteous, but sinners to repentance; — to seek the outcasts of society — harlots, publicans, and thieves.[50]

The responsibility for Primitive Methodist missionary work in north Lincolnshire was moved from Hull and centred on Market Rasen when Thomas King was appointed to work in the area as a travelling preacher in June 1819. In October of that year he preached in Grimsby and Clee.[51] By 1820 thirty-four regular preaching places had been established, extending south into the Louth area.[52] From Louth preachers moved out into the villages of the Marsh and southern Lincolnshire Wolds.[53]

In the early stages of Primitive Methodist activity in south Lincolnshire places such as Newark, Balderton and Harby, which were over the county boundary in Nottinghamshire, were centres for missionary work. Spittlegate, a manufacturing suburb of Grantham, was the only place in south Lincolnshire to appear on the connexion's preaching plan in May 1818. Services were held every fortnight at 2 p.m. on Sundays.[54] Societies began to be formed in villages on the Lincolnshire side of the boundary with Nottinghamshire such as the one at Norton Disney which was established after a visit by two female preachers.[55] William Clowes and John Wedgwood preached in the open air on Castle Hill in Lincoln in 1818, although it is possible that John Hallsworth had preceded them since their visit to the city was carefully planned and had been announced a fortnight in advance. Before they went to Lincoln they attended a camp meeting which had been arranged at the village of Wellingore.[56] Their efforts produced converts from outside Lincoln who became the basis for further expansion of the work.[57]

After the visit of Clowes and Wedgwood the Primitive Methodist community in Lincoln developed enough to begin to attract the attention of the local press. It was reported in December 1818 that the day of Queen Charlotte's funeral 'the occasion was made use of by the fraternity of Ranters, who have for some time past made a practice of performing their religious exercises in the public streets of Lincoln and neighbourhood.'[58] In the course of 1819 they were also reported as singing hymns at a public execution and organising a camp meeting to the north of the city where a large crowd, reported to be between two and three thousand strong 'principally composed of farmers' labourers, with a large proportion of women and children', joined in the 'exercises of the day . . . consisting of praying, singing and exhortation'. The activities at the camp meeting were said to be:

> diversified; consisting of praying, singing or exhortation. The praying was conducted at times by individuals, who took the lead alternately; and at other times, the whole of the more active members of the fraternity were engaged together, working upon each other's enthusiasm, and presenting to the astonished ears of the passengers whom chance or curiosity brought to the spot, a very Babel of broken exclamation with 'cries and groans, and shrieks that rent the air'.[59]

Indoor meetings were held in private houses until a chapel was opened in Lincoln in 1819. This was provided by a member of the local society but 'his conduct becoming such that he could not continue, the chapel, being private property, was lost' and a schoolroom capable of seating a hundred people was taken in Mint Lane.[60] The opening services of the first chapel were said to have 'presented a scene seldom witnessed, perhaps never equalled' in the city:

> The principal speakers on this occasion, after having worked themselves up to a state of the utmost phrensy, were succeeded by such of their brethren as felt themselves moved for the purpose. At the close of the evening, a circle being formed, and two girls whom the Ranters had converted being upon their knees within it, five or six of these enthusiasts began loudly to harangue at the same time. What with the confusion arising from this circumstance, the cries and groans of the infatuated followers of the sect, and the noise of the others who were collected to see them, a tumult arose which defies all description: happily it was allayed without the violent and desperate consequences which those without the walls fully expected from the disorder within. It is truly lamentable to witness the baneful effects which this ranting fraternity has produced upon the lower class of society . . .[61]

In March 1819 W. Wildbur and a female preacher named Perry were appointed to work in the city of Lincoln and among the Primitive Methodist societies and preaching places which had been established by then in the vicinity of the city. The camp meeting which Clowes and Wedgwood had held in Wellingore before they preached in Lincoln in 1818 had probably led to a class being formed in the village.[62] The travelling preacher John Harrison met it in January 1819 before going on to Lincoln.[63] In February he returned with his wife Sarah to open a new chapel in the village.[64] The couple also preached in Navenby where there were some Primitive Methodist families and, on Tuesday 9 February, they were in Lincoln where they joined a preacher who was going out to Washingborough. A meeting was held in a house there at which Sarah Harrison preached and, after returning to Lincoln, they were at Washingborough Fen on 12 February. After holding more meetings and preaching in Lincoln the Harrisons returned to

Nottinghamshire.[65]

Wildbur claimed that 'the Lord raised up many societies' during the period he worked in Lincoln but there is little positive evidence of this. After a few months he moved on to Boston where he may have worked with a preacher called Moss who had entered the town with others in 1819.[66] A society was established in Boston after much opposition and Wildbur also preached to the north in Wainfleet and Friskney.[67] Much of the work of establishing Primitive Methodism in south Lincolnshire at this period was done by John Hallsworth in the Lincoln circuit. This was created in September 1820 out of the area previously covered by the circuit based on Nottingham. Together with William Doughty and Francis Birch, Hallsworth covered considerable distances on preaching expeditions.[68] He preached at Heighington (where two early converts soon became local preachers), Fulbeck and Rowston. Doughty ranged widely across the county from villages to the north-west down to the south of Lincoln where he preached at a camp meeting at Rauceby. In late September 1820 he was at Wilsford and a place described as Swaby — probably the village of either Swaton or Swarby.[69] Francis Birch also worked in the Boston area in 1820 preaching regularly in Boston and Fishtoft as well as to 'several hundreds in the market place at Donnington [*sic*]'. He also preached at Aslackby and Rippingale, which in their turn became bases for further work in the area so that when he went to Haconby, 'a dark place', some of the 'friends' from these villages went with him.[70]

A camp meeting was held at Spalding on Sunday 1 October, but it was not the first visit of Primitive Methodist preachers to the area since Birch referred in his journal to a revival of the work in the town. Similarly, when he preached at Holbeach in the following week he entered a town where 'our preachers have been used ill' in the past. He then moved on to one of the Suttons, where again there had been preaching earlier, before returning to Boston and joining W. Wildbur there. Preaching was also reported in the villages of Butterwick and Whaplode. As a result of his work a society had been established at Spalding by late November 1820 and a prayer meeting was reported as being held at Whaplode at the same period.[71] After the December quarterly business meeting (see Glossary) at Boston Francis Birch wrote:

truly the presence of the Lord did crown our meeting. The
preachers, both travelling and local, appeared to be of one
heart, and one mind. And, glory to God, it rejoiced my soul
to hear how the work of God is reviving all over the circuit.
The Lord is pouring out his Holy Spirit in a wonderful
manner.[72]

In the area to the immediate south of Lincoln Primitive
Methodists had preached at Washingborough in 1819, where
Sarah Harrison had also addressed a house meeting at the time of
the village feast.[73] By 1820 preachers had also visited Branston and
established a flourishing society there.[74] John Prestwood, who
lived on Branston Moor about a mile from the village, invited the
Primitive Methodist preachers to his house at Christmas 1819. He
had been 'awakened' during preaching at Bardney, but his
connections were with Potter Hanworth where the Primitives first
preached in 1820. Prestwood later built a chapel in the village
which was handed over to the connexion in 1838.[75] Bassingham, a
village to the west of Lincoln towards the border with
Nottinghamshire, was another place visited by the Primitives in
this early phase of their activity, but it was later abandoned by
them until 1839.[76] On the other hand some villages where an early
presence was established remained committed to Primitive
Methodism. Timberland was first visited about 1820 when Samuel
Toynbee joined the connexion and 'for more than thirty years he
was a bright ornament to the little church meeting in his house. He
was delighted to see his cottage crowded with attentive hearers.'[77]
The journal of W. Fieldsend for the period January to February
1821 shows the wide geographical area he covered while working
on the Lincoln circuit, preaching at places as far apart as
Donington in the south of Lincolnshire and Minting, a village to
the north-west of Horncastle.[78] By the summer of 1821 he had
been joined by three other preachers.[79] Fieldsend seems to have
been active in the Lincoln area in June and July 1821, when, after
visiting the city for a quarterly meeting, he preached at Welbourn,
Waddington, and later at Heckington. Here he 'found them not in
such a flourishing state as I expected'. He also noted continuing
persecution of the Primitives at Waddington and Welbourn while
in December 1821 a farm servant at Wellingore was charged with
disturbing Primitive Methodist worship in the village but further
proceedings against him were stopped 'on his paying a guinea to

the poor of the parish and making a public acknowledgement of his offence'.[80] A large camp meeting was held on Canwick Common on 17 June 1821, on the Saturday before the quarterly meeting, and Fieldsend noted that 'thousands flocked to hear the word', while a newspaper report estimated the number present at 'between 2 and 3,000'.[81] The work of Fieldsend and his colleagues led to a growth in Primitive Methodist activity over a wide area and 'the good work prospered at Horncastle, Donnington [*sic*], Heckington, . . . and other places.'[82] Six preachers had also been sent to work in the Boston area in May 1821 although, according to one of them, J. Oscroft, 'there was not sufficient work for two'. They 'therefore opened a mission in the county of Norfolk, where the work of the Lord spread rapidly and hundreds were soon converted to God.'[83]

By the summer of 1821, according to a preaching plan which survives for the period, the Lincoln circuit had fifty-seven places where Sunday services were held regularly, extending into north Lincolnshire, taking in Horncastle and villages in the area as well as places to the north and west of Lincoln together with parts of Nottinghamshire. Twenty-three of them — Branston and Branston Moor, Washingborough, Heighington, Wellingore, Scredington, Heckington, Ruskington, Timberland, Walcott, Rowston, Norton Disney, Bassingham, Hougham, Claypole, Wilsford, Swarby, Sleaford, Rauceby, Beckingham, Leadenham, Fulbeck, Frieston and Normanton — were in south Lincolnshire with Lincoln at the head of the circuit. Few, if any of them, apart from Lincoln and Wellingore, had purpose-built chapels at this stage while the rest were, like the group at Samuel Toynbee's house in Timberland, meeting in cottages and private houses.[84] These congregations were served by four travelling preachers and three others, probably hired local preachers (see Glossary under Local Preacher), one of whom was a woman. Their listing in this order on the plan implies a hierarchy which distinguished not only between those who were full-time paid ministers and those who were not, but also between the various grades of unpaid lay preachers. It was an order which became clearer as the connexion developed.

The bulk of the Sunday preaching arrangements were undertaken by twenty-eight local preachers, twelve exhorters, a group described as 'Co' (Company) and an un-named person or

persons denoted by an asterisk.[85] Only Lincoln and Wellingore
had two Sunday services while the rest had one either weekly or
fortnightly. In addition, the full-time preachers took week-night
services once a fortnight in all the places on the plan except
Lincoln, where there were weekly meetings. These carefully-
planned week-night services served the inner core of Primitive
Methodist membership. They provided the means whereby the
full-time preachers were kept in contact with meetings of local
officials and the weekly class meetings of the local societies which
were the spiritual heart of the Primitive Methodist connexion. At
the class meetings each member stated 'with simplicity their
religious experience, and the various dealings of God with them'
while the class leaders gave 'such advice, instructions, etc. to each
of them as their state may require'. As well as supervising an
individual's spiritual life, the class meeting encouraged members
to turn their backs on worldly pastimes and provided a means of
supervising individual moral conduct.[86]

*   *   *   *   *   *

The growth and development of the Primitive Methodist
connexion's organisation which can be seen in the Lincoln plan
was not, however, reflected in the number of converts which were
made. The Lincoln circuit grew from 655 to 664 members between
1822 and 1823, an increase of 1 per cent compared with one of
nearly 18 per cent in the whole connexion. This was not because
the circuit's activities were curtailed. There were four travelling
preachers employed in 1822 and six in 1823. The growth in the
number of travelling preachers nationally was also not matched by
increased membership since the number of travelling preachers
increased by 33 per cent from 152 to 202.[87]

A camp meeting, held at Lincoln in June 1822, attracted 'several
hundred persons' compared with the larger attendance at a similar
meeting the year before and it was noted that, 'These enthusiasts,
from some cause or other, seem to have declined in public interest
in our neighbourhood.'[88] Changes in the boundary of the Lincoln
circuit are a partial explanation of a 49 per cent drop in its
membership to 338 in 1824, while the number of ministers also
went down to three.[89] There are no membership figures available
for Boston, which had grown out of Lincoln, at this period, while

Balderton in Nottinghamshire became the head of a circuit stretching into south Lincolnshire in 1824. It also took members away from Lincoln in that part of the county. The Grantham area was covered by Nottingham circuit until 1825 — although Lincoln-based preachers were working near Grantham in 1822. In that year a room was fitted up for preaching in the town and, together with Aslackby, Edenham and Rippingale, it became a separate mission (see Glossary).[90]

In 1825 and 1826 no membership figures for circuits were published — a reflection of the 'depression and crisis' which the connexion underwent during this period. There was some expansion in the north and west of the country, but the south Lincolnshire area experienced a loss of members or at best a static situation in common with other parts of the connexion.[91] The signs of this approaching crisis were apparent in the slow-down in the growth of membership in south Lincolnshire from 1822 compared with the greater rate of increase in the number of full-time ministers. This increase in preachers meant that the standards of candidates for the ministry fell and people were admitted 'who proved to be a burden, and, in some instances a curse rather than a blessing' so that 'societies languished under their inefficient labours, and even once flourishing circuits became feeble'.[92]

These problems were symptomatic of the difficulties which had been created by the rapid growth of the Primitive Methodist connexion. A wave of revivalistic fervour had carried the new organisation forward. The work of evangelists like John Benton had produced many converts, but since he and men and women like him 'paid very little attention to forming classes, and to introducing rule and order' the institutional structures which had sustained their work were relatively weak.[93] A period of tighter control, with a greater emphasis on building secure institutions on which to base the work of the connexion, followed the collapse and retreat of the crisis years of 1824 to 1828. Until circuit membership figures appear again on a regular basis from 1827 it is difficult to build up a picture of Primitive Methodism in south Lincolnshire. Places where a presence had been established as early as 1818 or 1819 were lost and it was necessary to carry out missionary work in them again. On the other hand there was continuity over the period in villages such as Claypole and Timberland.[94]

III

Ranter Preaching

The successes achieved by Primitive Methodist preachers in south Lincolnshire were based on their ability to relate to and provide a relevant religious dimension to the lives of country workers at a time when rapid social change was eroding older values and attitudes. Fears which were expressed about their potential to stir up disaffection illustrated the way in which they were caught up in the social tensions of the period. These were expressed by a clergyman living in the Spalding area in 1820 who set the connexion's roving preachers alongside other agents of social unrest:

> In times when the heralds of disaffection and emissaries of republicanism with revolutionary principles, are traversing the country in all directions, 'with good words and fair speeches, deceiving the hearts of the simple'; when runagates and vagabonds are feeling the national pulse, and agitating the public mind with impunity; when, under the specious pretext of religion, the peace of society is disturbed, mobs are collected, and great numbers of the lowest rabble concentrated by imposing novelties, upon the approach of evening; when the vitals of our excellent constitution are mangled through the sides of our Established Church; when schism, sedition and blasphemy, combine to raise their brazen crest, stalking through the kingdom, and unfurling their factious banners in every corner of the island; when the Church is openly assailed by an organized banditti of strolling Methodists, vociferating Ranters, and all that impious train of *et coeteras* [*sic*], who without either the substance or form of Christianity, nestle under the wings of, toleration, and hurl defiance at all constituted authorities. . .[1]

The ability of early Primitive Methodist preachers to speak plainly and in an idiom which could be understood by the people to whom they preached was seen as a vital asset. It was said as late as 1848 that the sort of education which made a man unfit to speak

46

to the most illiterate congregation was not suitable for a Primitive Methodist minister.[2] John Oxtoby's full-time preaching career with the Primitives began in north Lincolnshire in 1821 at a time when 'the work to which the early Primitive Methodist preachers were called in the order of Providence was mostly of a kind which did not require much learning, and little or no polish or refinement.'[3] His sermons were 'often crude' while in 'his pronunciation and attitude, he was uncouth', as he 'had no wish to add to his strong faith, ceaseless prayer, and deep piety, those mental stores which embellish the man, expand and refine the minds of the Christian, and give increasing qualification and sweetness to the zealous and powerful preacher.'[4]

Female preachers such as Ann Carr, Sarah Healand and Sarah Kirkland linked early Primitive Methodism to the domestic lives of the rural workers of south Lincolnshire by helping to assert the role of women in providing a refuge against the stresses of social change through a religious experience rooted in the home.[5] Women like Grace Meadows of Rippingale, who died in 1828, were able to play a key role in early Primitive Methodism by opening 'an effectual door for the preaching of the gospel' in their houses.[6] The life of Mrs Elizabeth Moore, who died at Welby near Grantham in 1869 at the age of eighty illustrated how Primitive Methodism's appeal to women could help to meet the needs of both individuals and families in a changing and potentially harsh environment. In spite of the problems of holding her home together and bringing up three children during a widowhood of more than forty years, she was able to fulfil herself as a Primitive Methodist preacher until nearly the end of her life when she became so enfeebled that she had to sit to address 'a few words of piety to the people'.[7]

Open air preaching brought the Primitive Methodists into contact with large numbers of working people. A camp meeting held to the north of Lincoln in May 1819 attracted 'principally. . . farmers' labourers with a large proportion of women and children', while a similar occasion held at Caistor three months later was estimated as being attended by between three and four thousand people of whom the majority were 'farmers' servants, day-labourers, and village mechanics'.[8] These were boisterously enthusiastic occasions and the 'diversified' activities of the day at the Lincoln meeting consisted of:

praying, singing and exhortation. The praying was conducted at times by individuals, who took the lead alternately; and at other times, the whole of the more active members of the fraternity were engaged together, working upon each other's enthusiasm, and presenting to the astonished ears of the passengers whom chance or curiosity brought to the spot, a very Babel of broken exclamations, with 'cries and groans, and shrieks that rent the air'.[9]

The loose structure of the open air meetings was picked upon by hostile commentators:

their proceedings have a tendency to confusion, rather than order; some of their preachers are known to have led wicked lives; and even women, in their public harangues, conceal not from their hearers their former iniquities, but laying aside all bashfulness, proclaim the baseness of their previous lives. To such a pitch of frenzy are they at times wound up, that their gesture and actions assimilate nearer to the orgies of the Heathen, than to the dignified deportment and calm devoutness of the Christian worshipper.[10]

The atmosphere was carried over into indoor worship when enthusiasm was the main qualification for participation, bringing a vitality which was denied to the congregations of conventional churches and chapels.[11] It included prayers:

consisting of violent ejaculations, familiar and repeated invocations of the name of Jesus, rapturous exclamations uttered with such clamour as if heaven were to be opened by their loud speaking, [which] must readily be conceived to be as distant as possible from that humility, sober-mindedness, and lowly adoration of soul and body, which becomes sinful men in their addresses to the throne of Grace.[12]

Yet the success of the Primitive Methodists depended ultimately on their ability to make converts from out of the crowds who were attracted to their meetings. There was no doubt that the acceptance of the message of their preachers, no matter how popular the tone or the means by which it was delivered, meant that it was necessary for an individual to put aside old habits. The fear of the Lord, according to a sermon of 1822, brought a life centred on hearth, home and the chapel. Those who feared the Lord did not:

> expose themselves to many dangers from drinking, wrestling, fighting, bull baiting, cock fighting, horse racing and many similar evils; all of which are calculated to injure the health and sink the soul into an everlasting hell, which burneth with fire and brimstone.[13]

A man who followed the way offered by the Primitive Methodists, it was said, brought positive benefits on himself and his family. He was able to provide them with the necessaries and conveniences of life and in doing it was 'not injured with excesses nor distressed with more want than is good for his soul'.[14] Until their conversion many Primitive Methodists were said to have followed 'wild courses'. They attended 'places of public amusements', were 'fond of the fashions and amusements of this present evil world', delighted in 'the abominations which are in the world' and added 'fresh vices to their former ones; and in the latter, rioting with increased ardour'.[15]

The old habits of converts were not always 'the grosser immoralities, such as drunkenness, &c.'[16] James Burwell of Little London, near Spalding, lived, 'according to the course of this world' yet 'did not relish gross scenes of vice, but was of a steady and thoughtful turn'.[17] It was said of William Bailey of Norton Disney that he was:

> of a gay turn of mind, and fond of the pleasures of this life. He was likewise particularly fond of music; which . . . in minds like his, has a peculiar tendency to drown every serious thought, as it generally brings them into the company with such as are trifling with their precious souls; and who, whilst they are pursuing after vain objects, are making light of everything which is calculated to inspire the mind with seriousness.[18]

The opposition which early Primitive Methodist preachers faced in effecting these conversions was not confined to derisory reports in the local press. It also involved active persecution including physical violence, the form and content of which emphasised the extent to which Primitive Methodism was a challenge to past patterns of behaviour. A generalised account, which conflated several elements of the type of persecution the Primitives might meet, described early Primitive Methodist activity in a village. After a preliminary visit it would be announced that there would be a visit by a preacher the next week:

> The day arrived, and the missionary appeared . . . every arrangement had been made for his reception . . . the eggs are thrown . . . while he proceeds with his service . . . The eggs being exhausted, the 'rough music' is brought to play upon him, and the throng now gather round him. Some blow their wind instruments, and others beat with sticks those of a drum kind . . . Those who had no instruments, united as they could in adding to the tumult and uproar . . . But other, and much more injurious weapons than those have often been employed. Blood from the slaughter house, thrown over the missionary . . . eggs charged with vitriol, and other injurious ingredients . . . Ropes, and even chains, to run round the missionary and his friends, and thereby drag them into some contiguous water or slough. The excrement of cattle, and other things, have not been found too loathsome for these poor misguided creatures to employ on these occasions. These humiliating scenes normally closed by the greater part of the mob following the missionary out of the place, and pelting him with stones, or flints for the road.[19]

This crowd action was almost always conservative in its goals and used the forms of traditional communal pastimes to demonstrate its adherence to the *status quo*.[20] John Hallsworth described how, when preaching in the Lincoln area in 1818, he was: 'almost continually in danger of [his] life. Mobs were raised up at almost every place. Eggs were flying, together with stones and dirt! — Cocks were fighting; — bells were ringing; — men were drinking and smoking, and holding up their hats and hallooing.'[21]

The persecution of the Primitive Methodist was one of the last phases of traditional crowd action in support of collective goals. Crowds did come together to protest about narrower and more intensely personal issues of moral behaviour throughout the rest of the nineteenth century, but they ceased to articulate real social grievances. Only individual and clandestine acts such as incendiarism and animal maiming were left as vehicles of protest for the working classes of south Lincolnshire from the 1830s until the development of trade unions in the 1870s. The Primitive Methodists offered as an alternative the experience of personal salvation and the means of spiritual and social development for the individual within the institutions created by the connexion. So it was as agents of change — 'the heralds of the coming day' — that they were 'cursed' and attacked.[22]

Individuals who followed their way and gained salvation were provided with a basis for life in the new social order which was developing in south Lincolnshire. Their souls were saved in a dramatic clash between the forces of good and evil in which they assumed a supreme importance as they sought to triumph over Satan. This struggle was carried on within a framework of language and imagery which was meaningful to them and it was the ability of the Primitive Methodists to link their teachings to popular beliefs which cemented their relationship with the working classes.

The wide range of these beliefs extended well beyond the bounds of orthodox Christian teaching. They had no distinct form or pattern which was peculiar to Lincolnshire, nor did they form a coherent structure which offered a comprehensive doctrine or view of the world or an explanation of human existence.[23] They were said to be still tenaciously held in the Lincolnshire countryside during the nineteenth century and to be as real 'as the fact of the Reformation or the Battle of Waterloo'. The way in which they came to be less central to the lives of all except the working classes is seen in the reports which emphasised the lowly social position of those who still adhered to popular beliefs and superstitions and how they became related increasingly to the private lives of individuals rather than matters of public concern.[24]

The collections of folklore material on which any assessment of popular beliefs has to be based were gathered at different times, for differing purposes and using different systems of classification. This makes it difficult to assess any changes which took place in the actual content of popular beliefs in the course of the nineteenth century.[25] It seems, however, that at least those elements survived which had the function of helping individuals to overcome or come to terms with moments of crisis in their lives and to give them points of reference and possible explanations for the problems which they faced. These also included the events surrounding birth, adolescence, marriage and death.

Early Primitive Methodist preachers were receptive to these popular beliefs.[26] Hugh Bourne and William Clowes were convinced of the power of witches and of dreams and visions. They were nurtured in this by their early contact with James Crawfoot the illiterate leader of the Magic Methodists of Delamere Forest in Cheshire.[27] A writer on 'The Church in Lincolnshire' showed how the values and attitudes of local preachers provided a sound basis for preaching among the 'agricultural poor' which was said to 'abound in relations of dreams and visions, and supposed supernatural or semi-supernatural . . . events, which the poor, we may say with truth, universally accept and believe'.[28]

One strong element in popular belief which was of great importance to the Primitive Methodists was the Devil.[29] Even if God or Christ were remote or often talismatic figures, he was very real, appearing in dreams or visions and in one case being the agent of the conversion of a drunken man to Methodism.[30] Primitive Methodist preachers struggling for the salvation of individual souls met and overcame what they saw as personal manifestations of the devil using language and imagery which were meaningful to their converts. Grace Meadows of Rippingale, who died in January 1828, had been depressed by Satan at the loss of her only son two years before. However, when she was confined to her bed during her final illness her 'faith was brought into vigorous exercise. Hope at once gained an ascendancy over unbelief; . . . Satan stood aloof in the hour of triumph!'[31] After what was described as 'a severe conflict' with the devil:

> she again caught hold of her Redeemer, and patiently waited the hour of her removal to a better world. Methinks I see throngs of vanquished infernals rushing back to the dark territories of hell in the greatest confusion and disorder! while bending angels are hovering over the death-bed of an expiring sister, anxiously waiting for the last gasp, and to bear the triumphant conqueror to her native heaven[32]. . .

Satan was said to have been bruised under the feet of Sarah, another member of the Meadows family of Rippingale, during her last illness. She triumphed over 'the world, the flesh, and the devil,' while when William Dale of Aisby lay dying 'Satan did not give up the contest as the dying Christian approached the grave, still the Captain of our salvation gave support in battle, and finally enabled the worn-out warrior to tread on the neck of his adversary.'[33] Similarly, during the last illness of Pidd White of Fulbeck: 'the powers of darkness assailed him keenly, but he conquered through faith in the blood of the Lamb. A short period before his death, Satan made his final attack; but through prayer and faith in the merits of the Redeemer, our brother gained the victory.'[34]

After the individual had triumphed over Satan and the powers of darkness Primitive Methodism built on this experience to give a more coherent view of life and the hereafter than was to be found in traditional folk beliefs and which provided him or her with the basis for understanding their place in the new social order which developed in south Lincolnshire in the nineteenth century. In the bliss of heaven — the ultimate goal of the convert — those who were saved finally gained a pattern and meaning to their lives which had seemed to be denied them as a result of the pressures of social change. Heaven brought the apotheosis of the convert's life on earth — a heaven made comprehensible by literal descriptions of its qualities. Images of trade, treasure and commerce emphasised how the dead person made gains which were denied to them in their earthly life, so that the happy spirit, released by death, exchanged poverty for riches and pain for pleasure while death became 'a gainful merchandise' in which hunger and thirst were driven away.[35] The family, divided by death in their earthly life, could be reunited in heaven so that, according to the north Lincolnshire Primitive Methodist minister J.R. Parkinson: 'in that multitude what saint has not a friend or relative, a brother or sister, a father or mother, a partner or child, waiting to hail him welcome to the better land — to show him where the living fountains play, and the trees of life do bloom.'[36]

In a death bed exhortation to her friends 'to be faithful' Martha Knott of Branston 'said she had no doubt of meeting them in heaven. When her dissolution drew nigh, she said to her mother: "I am going to meet my friends that are gone before, and you will soon follow me."'[37] Similarly, Mary Robinson of Claypole hoped eventually to meet her husband and nine children in heaven and, she exhorted them on her deathbed 'not to seek for happiness in this world; but prepare to meet her in heaven'.[38] In her old age Elizabeth Prestwood spoke of 'the approaching period when she should unite with many who had already gone to the better land, and others who would soon follow, and whom she had esteemed on earth.'[39] The ideal earthly life would be created in heaven so that, although William White left behind the chapel services which he loved to attend when he died early on a Sunday morning at Lincoln, he joined a higher form of this when 'his happy soul escaped from its emaciated tabernacle, and went to spend an eternal Sabbath with the heavenly worshippers in the temple on high.'[40]

The link between heaven and earth was strengthened by the foretaste of heaven which was frequently vouchsafed to the dying. William Brown, a local preacher from Ewerby, had 'a remarkable vision' in which: 'he saw the glory of the New Jerusalem, and his daughter, who died about eight months before, surrounded with a blaze of dazzling light. "Bless the Lord", said he afterwards to a friend, "my daughter is now in glory, and I shall soon be with her."'[41]

Yet, if these descriptions made heaven comprehensible and desirable to the people who were converted by the Primitive Methodists, it was only through conversion that these rewards were obtainable. The unconverted were warned that in the afterlife:

> *Your employment,* instead of singing salvation with the white-robed multitude in heaven, will be to gaze on terrific forms, to listen to frightful sounds, to breath sulphurous air, and to roll in liquid fire, where the prospect of eternal woe fills the mind with constant horror. Would you escape this agony? repent of sin, pray for pardon, believe in Christ, 'wash and be clean'.[42]

Without conversion the hell of broken relationships and of disrupted social and domestic ties resulting from death, mobility and social change would be perpetuated after death:

> friend will witness against friend. Pious parents will witness against ungodly children. There stands that ungodly son, that

wicked daughter, trembling before the Judge, confounded by
the testimony of mother and father . . .
Pious children will witness against their parents. Ungodly
children will witness against their parents. My father never
taught me the fear of the Lord. My father taught me to swear
and to get drunk, my mother to lie and break the Sabbath.
The husband will witness against the wife and the wife against
the husband, the sister against the brother and the brother
against the sister, the mother against the daughter and the
daughter against the mother, ministers against their people
and the people against their ministers.

Let not the ungodly husband think that he can cling to the
garments of his pious wife, and thus be introduced to the
favour of the Judge. Those pious members of your family on
earth, that now pray and weep before God for your salvation,
cannot help you then. . .

See children separated from their parents. Families interred
in one tomb, see how they are now separated, sundered for
ever. Oh! how they shriek as they sink into the infernal gulf.
What dreadful cries of despair![43]

Primitive Methodism brought the hope of deliverance through
the experience of conversion to individuals buffetted by the
circumstances of the world. All could be made new in the life to
come, but more was needed than mere outward conformity as was
made clear by the Lincolnshire preacher Parkinson Milson when
he pointed out that it was not sufficient to be 'outwardly moral'. A
man could be 'a good husband or neighbour' and 'possess
aimiable instincts and affections, and do many praiseworthy
deeds' and yet 'be as void of holiness as the openly profane'.[44] The
deep emotional change which conversion brought gave an
individual a sense of worth and value in a changing world. This
experience was the basis on which the Primitives built up an
organisation which sustained their converts and carried their work
forward in the villages of south Lincolnshire.

IV

Chapel Life

The state of Primitive Methodism in south Lincolnshire as it emerged from the period of crisis which affected it between 1824 and 1828 can be gauged from a set of returns of non-Anglican places of worship which were made in June 1829 covering 184 settlements in the Kesteven division of south Lincolnshire.[1] The Primitives had ten places of worship in Norton Disney, Caythorpe with Frieston, Fulbeck, Hougham, Westborough, Martin, Rippingale, Edenham with Grimsthorpe, Elsthorpe and Scottlethorpe, and Welby. This made them the second largest non-Anglican religious organisation in the area after the Wesleyan Methodists who had sixty-three meetings out of a total of ninety-five. All the Primitive Methodist congregations met in houses, except those at Fulbeck, Hougham and Martin where there were chapels. A group of 'Protestant Wesleyan Methodists, formerly Ranters' met in a chapel at Claypole built for the Primitive Methodists which later came back into their possession.[2]

Without a chapel building given over to their use the long-term position of the Primitive Methodists, or indeed any Nonconformist body, could be precarious. In a closed village the landlord could exert a powerful influence on their ability to build. Until the Earl of Dysart consented to grant a piece of land to the Primitive Methodists at Great Ponton they could not build a chapel in which to hold their services but used a small cottage up to 1858.[3] When the foundation stone of Burton Coggles Primitive Methodist chapel was laid in 1870 the Revd T.S. Whitehead complained in his address of 'landed proprietors who objected to grant sites of land on which to erect places of Dissenting worship'.[4]

Only three of the places where the Primitives were established in 1829 still had a place of worship of any sort by the time of the 1851 Census of Religious Worship. These were at Fulbeck, Martin and Rippingale, of which Fulbeck and Martin had chapels in 1829.[5] All of them were in open villages. However, in spite of the fact that by 1829 the Primitives had established meetings in closed villages like Edenham, part of the Ancaster estate, where some ten or a dozen

56

Ranters were said to hold prayer meetings in a private room, they were unable to sustain their position there. By 1851, when there were fifty-six Primitive Methodist places of worship in the whole of south Lincolnshire, the number of chapels had increased to forty-one, while fifteen congregations met in houses. Thirty-nine of the chapels and eleven of the house meetings were in open villages. This shift in the centres of Primitive Methodist activity cannot simply be accounted for by the fact that the 1851 figures include the Holland division of south Lincolnshire, for which there are no surviving returns from 1829. Even in the area covered by the 1829 returns in Kesteven there were twenty-eight sites with Primitive Methodist places of worship in 1851 of which twenty-two were in open villages. Fifteen of these were in purpose-built chapels, three of which were in closed villages. There were seven house meetings in open and three in closed villages, so although the cottage meeting remained a significant part of Primitive Methodist life, helping to maintain activities in many villages, the main thrust of the connexion's activities had by 1851 begun to be based in chapels in open villages. The development of Primitive Methodism became increasingly tied to the maintenance and development of secure institutional structures in these places, after its first wide-ranging and charismatic phase of activity had ended in the period of collapse from 1824 to 1828.

The development of Primitive Methodism in Rauceby had 'been impeded for want of a larger place of worship' until a new chapel was opened in October 1834.[6] At Holbeach Bank 'the cause had suffered, and was likely to suffer, for want of a convenient place to rest the ark of the Lord' until a chapel was opened in 1835, while the prospects for Primitive Methodism in Whaplode became 'very encouraging' after a chapel was opened in 1836.[7] Chapel building was seen to bring signs of Divine favour which sanctioned the step the local society had taken. 'The presence of the Lord was felt in a very peculiar manner' and 'the divine glory overshadowed us, and the shout of triumph ascended to the skies' when Donington chapel opened on Christmas Day 1834. The first services at Gosberton Clough chapel three months later were described as 'a powerful time'.[8] The conversions which marked the opening of the new chapel at Martin in July 1837 were a sign that 'the spirit of God accompanied his word of grace.' This atmosphere spilled over into the week-night services held in the

Fig.4 Centres of Primitive Methodist activity in south Lincolnshire distinguishing between open and closed villages.

village and spread a spirit of revival into the neighbourhood. It was reported that 'several souls were convinced of sin, and one, on the Monday evening, professed to obtain peace with God . . . and two more on the Tuesday evening at Timberland.'[9]

The acquisition of a chapel brought the Primitive Methodists into a more central place in village life and the outward characteristics of a chapel were seen as a reflection of the status of the community who worshipped in it. The 'very commodious building, greatly admired by the public for strength and neatness' at Donington was said to reflect much credit on its builders.[10] The building of a chapel in 1838 at Freiston Shore, a bathing resort about four miles outside Boston which was 'much resorted to in summer by the people of Boston, and other places', filled a gap in the religious provision of the area. It was the only place of worship of any sort within two miles of the resort and so became a significant part of the local religious scene, attracting people to worship who had come to bathe. In this way it gained middle- and upper-class patronage in raising money for the building.[11] The importance of chapels in Primitive Methodist development after 1828 was reflected in the number which were built. Twenty-one of the forty-one chapels enumerated in the 1851 Census of Religious Worship dated from the 1830s and the largest number in any one year were the five built in 1834, followed by four in 1839.[12]

It is difficult to relate this activity to variations in the local membership of the connexion because of changes in circuit boundaries since circuits based outside south Lincolnshire included places in south Lincolnshire, and south Lincolnshire circuits contained places outside the area. However, membership of south Lincolnshire circuits, which was 418 in 1829, increased rapidly from 1832, when there were 467 members. There were 665 in 1833 and the number reached 1067 in 1836. After some fluctuations it began to rise again to a peak of 1183 in 1842, followed by a period of decline until 1848 when membership began to grow again and increased from 1210 to 1549 in 1851.

Primitive Methodist worship was attended by more than members but it was not until the 1851 Census of Religious Worship that there is any significant measure of attendances. By this time the increase in the number of chapels built had moved the connexion from its cottage-based sectarian origins into a more central role in village life. The Sunday worship at the chapel together with the associated week-night activities was becoming part of the general pattern of village social activities, enhancing the role of the Primitives as they became another centre for recreation and entertainment as well as religious worship. Comparisons of the number of attenders and members can be best made at a local level. These show considerable variations from place to place, ranging from a proportion of 58 per cent of members at the best-attended Sunday service at Boston to as low as 5 per cent in the fenland community of Tydd Gote. They are, however, extremes and the average level of the proportion of attenders to members was in the region of 30 per cent, except in that part of the Wisbech circuit, including Tydd Gote, which covered the south Lincolnshire fens.[13] Here the comparatively small amount of accommodation provided by the Church of England meant that Nonconformist places of worship became relatively more important. People might attend them because alternatives were limited, so increasing the proportion of attenders at the expense of fully committed chapel members, whereas in other places they would go to the established church.[14]

The best attended Primitive Methodist services in south Lincolnshire on the day of the Religious Census of 1851, Sunday 30 March, were in the evening. A total of 3537 people, including those classed as Sunday scholars, were either actually counted at worship or, in places where a count was not made, were said to usually attend worship then. This was just sixteen less than the best attended service of the Baptist churches of the area, which were held on the Sunday morning. The largest attendances of all the churches were at the Church of England and the Wesleyan Methodists. The Church had 26,102 at its best service in the morning. The Wesleyans, like the Primitive Methodists attracted most people in the evening — 12,147 on 30 March.[15] These figures conceal significant variations within the area and in the Sleaford, Grantham, Lincoln and Newark registration districts the Primitives were clearly the third best-attended religious body after the Church of England and the Wesleyan Methodists. These districts covered the heathlands of south Lincolnshire as well as the western valley of Kesteven. Here larger farms were relatively more important and the contrast between open and closed villages was marked. The fenland areas of Boston, Holbeach and Spalding, which had nothing except open villages, were less polarised. The older dissenting churches, and especially the Baptists, supported by the small farmers and landowners whose presence gave the area its characteristic social structure, were well-established here.

Any idea of the actual composition of the congregations enumerated in the 1851 Census of Religious Worship must, however, be deduced from the ways in which the people attending church or chapel behaved on Census Sunday. The fact that the Primitive Methodists achieved their best attendances at evening service suggests that their adherents either waited until the end of a Sunday before going to chapel or that they attended services at other places of worship — perhaps the Church of England which had its best-attended services in the morning and slightly less well-attended services in the afternoon. People involved in heavy manual labour from Monday to Saturday might rest on Sunday morning. Alternatively the demands of livestock would also occupy the earlier part of the day. The Vicar of Wrangle attributed below average attendances at the time of the Census of Religious Worship to 'several persons having been engaged in looking after sheep, in this, the lambing season'. Among the factors which, according to the Rector of Swaby in north Lincolnshire, diminished attendance were the lambing season 'when the sheep require attendance day and night, and excessive fatigue of harvest to men, women and children.'[16] It was said that the small farmers and labourers of Thorpe on the Hill were obliged 'to be in the fields attending their lambs' on Census Sunday.[17]

Attendance by the same person at the services of more than one denomination and especially attendance at both the Anglican church and a Nonconformist chapel on the same Sunday was found in many areas in the nineteenth century. It was also noted in the 1851 Census of Religious Worship.[18] In the seven south Lincolnshire villages, where the Primitive Methodists provided the only alternative place of worship to the Church of England, they achieved their best attendances in all except one of these at a different time of the day to the church. This suggests that a group of people moved between church and chapel, attending both at different times of the day. It does not, however, exclude the possibility that the Primitives attracted people who were not able to attend at any other time of the day to their evening services when the Anglican churches were usually closed. This meant that the Primitives both attracted people who also attended the Church of England as well as having a following among people who were either only able or only willing to attend religious worship in the evening. Moreover, attendances at other Nonconformist chapels were also strong on a Sunday evening so that, whatever the problems in interpreting the evidence of the 1851 Census of Religious Worship, it shows that the Primitive Methodists had created a distinct set of adherents for themselves by 1851. Some of their attendants might be found in the village church at other times of the day, but to others the Primitive Methodist chapel would be the only place at which they worshipped.

Baptism registers give the occupations of the fathers of children who were brought to the Primitive Methodists for this rite and therefore show the social groups from which they attracted support. The registers of Lincoln, Boston, Spalding, Donington and Sleaford circuits survive for various dates between 1823 and 1873. After the baptisms of more than one child belonging to the same parents have been eliminated there are details of the occupations of 1992 fathers. The four largest groups of occupations were 901 labourers, 452 craftsmen, 152 tradesmen and 141 farmers.[19] However, this strong support for the Primitives among the working classes of south Lincolnshire needs to be qualified since the importance of baptism as a rite of passage rather than a religious sacrament meant that it might not necessarily be a strong indicator of religious allegiance in all cases. In the village of Springthorpe in north Lincolnshire the labourers of the parish were less strongly committed to one particular church than the farmers or craftsmen.[20] Where it was difficult to reach the parish church in some of the remote fenland settlements of south Lincolnshire then 'Methodism or nothing' was the only option open to parents and a significant number of the Primitive Methodist baptisms in south Lincolnshire were from outlying places.[21] None the less even where it was extremely difficult parents still went to considerable trouble to have their children baptised into the Church of England although, according to the Revd J. Tunstall Smith of Whaplode writing in 1845, they often seemed to value the rites and customs associated with the ceremony as much as any spiritual significance it had.[22]

However, labourers were not only passive recipients of the ministrations of the Primitive Methodist connexion. They also assumed a role as leaders of the local chapel community which was significant, even if comparatively less important, than their place in the registers. Seventeen title deeds for eleven chapels in south Lincolnshire in the period 1826 to 1875 contain details of the occupations of 154 chapel trustees[23](see Glossary). Forty-one or nearly 27 per cent were labourers, compared with 45 per cent of labourers' children in the baptism registers. On the other hand a greater proportion of farmers acted as trustees than had their children baptised by the Primitive Methodists. This may reflect the fact that the more senior and therefore older men in the congregations who assumed this position were less likely to have young children, but it is also necessary to be cautious about the status which should be accorded to the description 'farmer'. The forty-eight men described in this way, who comprised 31 per cent of trustees, were especially prominent in the trusts of fenland chapels where small farmers were a significant element in the local economy. In many places these men were said to be 'very little raised above the hired labourer' and in their younger days might not have yet attained the status of 'farmer'. This would help to explain the smaller proportion — 7 per cent — of the children of farmers appearing in the baptism registers. By the time a labourer attained the status of farmer his children had already been baptised.[24] Tradesmen and craftsmen appear in approximately the same proportions in the trusts and in the baptism registers as in the population as a whole. It is, however, the proportion of labourers on chapel deeds that is particularly significant. The proportion who acted as trustees reflects their numerical strength in local society, showing that the Primitive Methodist connexion was giving them the opportunity to play a part in its affairs as leaders and as office holders. This, together with the number of labourers' children baptised by the Primitive Methodists, is evidence of the extent of the connexion's identification with the rural workers of south Lincolnshire into the second half of the nineteenth century.

*   *   *   *   *   *

As the Primitive Methodists grew in numbers and their institutions became stronger they developed into a significant part of the social life of the local communities where they were established. Their

regular cycle of Sunday and week-night services, interspersed with
an annual round of special events such as Sunday school and
chapel anniversaries, became a well-established part of the social
scene in villages. Occasional extraordinary events in the life of the
local chapel community, such as the opening of a new building,
heightened the Primitives' profile. However, since what they did,
both as part of their normal provision as well as on special
occasions, differed little in its form and content from other
Nonconformist bodies and organisations they became very much
part of the texture of rural life.

Chapel events not only ministered to the spiritual needs of the
people who supported them, but also became the means whereby
the connexion's activities were maintained. The life of the local
Primitive Methodist community at Great Gonerby, near
Grantham, illustrates the place the local chapel came to occupy in
village life. In 1857 the foundation stone of a new chapel was laid
and the celebrations included a tea for a hundred and seventy
people in the Wesleyan chapel attended by 'the principal
inhabitants, with their labourers'. There was a public meeting in
the evening with six speakers and 'a larger congregation than has
been seen at Gonerby for some years past'.[25] Special meetings and
services were held in February of the next year to raise money for
the new chapel, attracting large numbers. Speakers included
Wesleyan and Methodist New Connexion ministers — a sign that
the Primitives were moving into a more central position in local
religious life. A local newspaper commented that, 'However the
Primitive Methodists might have been despised, it is evident that
there is a progression in intellect on the part of many of their
ministers.'[26] When the new chapel was completed its opening was
marked by sermons and meetings which also had a strong social
element, including two public teas and a lecture on 'the idolatrous
worship, customs and ceremonies prevalent in the East Indies,
illustrated by numerous diagrams'.[27]

The role the Primitive Methodists had come to occupy in village
life was illustrated by the way in which the new chapel building at
Great Gonerby was supported by 'the farmers and inhabitants of
the place generally, as well as several gentlemen in the
neighbourhood' so that it was no longer only the concern of the
group of converts who made up the village's Primitive Methodist
society.[28] This support was renewed and sustained by the cycle of

services and meetings based on the new chapel which also provided entertainment and recreation for a wider audience than regular chapel attenders.

One important element in these events was the annual Sunday school anniversary and the type of celebration which marked the first of them became an annual pattern:

> The Sunday school anniversary sermons were preached on Sunday last, by Mr. White of Bingham. The children recited some very nice pieces to a large congregation. The collections were good. On the following Monday the children had tea and afterwards the friends. The chapel was nicely decorated with flowers and suitable mottoes. The meeting in the evening was addressed by Messrs. White, Betts and Brodhead[29]. . .

The anniversary of the chapel opening was also celebrated each year by special sermons and a tea meeting. In 1865 many were unable to fit into the building for an evening lecture on Martin Luther.[30] The next year between three and four hundred people were reported as having attended the chapel anniversary tea which was followed by a lecture on 'The Young Man's hindrances to true greatness'.[31]

The increased numbers attracted by the activities in the new chapel of 1857 meant that extra accommodation was required. In 1863 the building was enlarged and improved, and a new schoolroom added. This created a further debt which in turn needed special services and events to reduce it. The opening of the improvements was marked by special services, a tea and a lecture on 'True Heroes' and, in the course of the next year, nearly £79 was raised to clean the chapel, build the new schoolroom and pay off £20 of the £120 debt remaining on the original chapel premises.[32] By 1873 it was said that there were insufficient sittings and a new building was opened in October of that year which led to another cycle of fund-raising activities to provide a further £330.[33]

Great Gonerby Primitive Methodist chapel also provided accommodation for the village's temperance society, whose meetings and public gatherings took a form very similar to those arranged by the Primitives themselves. The second anniversary of the temperance society had tea and public meetings together with recitations from the children of the Band of Hope.[34] The similarities between the type of meetings they held as well as, in the case of Great Gonerby, a common meeting place, helped to blur the distinction between the Primitive Methodists and other morally uplifting and improving activities — a further indication of the extent to which the Primitives had become assimilated into village life.

The mixture of social and religious activities which made up the life of a local Primitive Methodist community was underlain by the need to continue to raise money to support the connexion's institutions. As well as the maintenance of its full-time ministers and the activities of the local circuit and district within which a chapel was situated, the provision of a building in which these activities took place put a heavy burden on local societies. The initial cost of a building was frequently met by mortgaging the chapel and the land on which it was built. After the trustees of Little Hale chapel bought the land for it in 1836 at a cost of £10 they raised a mortgage on the land and chapel which was eventually discharged in December 1860.[35] These debts were often compounded by a local society deciding to rebuild or replace a chapel before the debt on the earlier building had been fully discharged. Leake in the Boston circuit had a mortgage of £217 on their chapel when it was built in 1839, but £65 of this was from an earlier building which it replaced.[36]

There was no apparent relationship between the size of the debt and the membership of the local Primitive Methodist society. Chapel debts on the Donington circuit in 1868 included £100 at South Kyme which had a society of only five members, while Gosberton Clough with eight members had the largest debt, £290, in the whole circuit. Donington's fifty-seven members supported a debt of £220. Nor did chapel debts necessarily decrease with time since the desire to replace or alter and enlarge old buildings was prevalent. Even if a society did not increase its commitments before the earlier ones were paid off it often happened that as soon as one debt was repaid it was replaced by another. After the society at Wrangle Bank had reduced the debt on their chapel from £45 in 1869 to £5 in 1874 they borrowed £100 to build a replacement.[37]

Debts were financed from a number of sources, including individuals, friendly societies and other chapels. Ancaster chapel was mortgaged with Rowland Williams of Sleaford at 5 per cent interest. He was described in the chapel deeds as a gentleman and had no obvious connections with the Primitive Methodists. The mortgage was transferred to C.E. Bissill, a Sleaford solicitor, in 1851 and when he called it in the debt was taken over by Francis Elliot, an Ancaster carpenter. In 1848 Helpringham chapel trustees obtained a mortgage from a group of local tradesmen and artisans who may have been Primitive Methodists.[38] At a later date money was raised to meet chapel debts by borrowing from friendly societies. When Boston's new chapel was being built in 1866 the trustees approached a Sleaford friendly society to borrow £500 while two of their members were also requested 'to inquire at their respective clubs to see if we can take some money up of them'. It was later agreed to borrow £300 'from the club at the Red Cow if we can have it on note'.[39] There was also some money-lending between chapels when surpluses were available. In June 1853 the Boston trustees lent £20 and £10 to two chapels in the Boston circuit.[40] However, since most chapels were usually in debt this cannot have been a significant element in their financial transactions.

The support of the work of the local circuit and of the Primitive Methodist connexion as a whole ultimately fell on its members. By the middle of the nineteenth century the framework of Primitive Methodist organisation in south Lincolnshire was in shape and the main centres of activity had been established. Membership in the area grew, with fluctuations, from the 1549 members in 1851 to 2454 by 1875, but this overall increase concealed considerable differences between circuits and a major part of this growth was in the city of Lincoln. The circuit based on the city and covering the surrounding countryside grew by 130 per cent from 312 in 1851 to a total of 719 by 1874. The fenland circuit of Donington had 281 members in 1851 but had dropped to 271 by 1875, whereas Boston circuit, which included the town of Boston, grew from 352 members in 1851 to 427 in 1875. The effect of membership levels on the financial strength of a circuit was seen by the fact that while Boston incurred a deficit on its quarterly accounts twenty-five times out of ninety-seven in the period December 1831 to December 1875, Donington had a deficit sixty-eight out of a possible eighty-nine times between 1858 and 1875. From 1860 Donington's circuit finances were usually in deficit. In the 1850s money was borrowed to meet the circuits' obligations when a shortfall occurred and another strategy was not to pay the travelling preachers' salaries in full.[41] The local societies in the Spalding and Holbeach area were organised as a branch, which meant that they had less automony than a circuit and were under the supervision of the Donington circuit from 1854 after a period under Wisbech. The branch either only balanced its quarterly accounts or showed a small surplus on nine occasions between September 1849 and December 1857 and it was in a state of continuous deficit between June 1853 and December 1857. From 1862 it was placed under the central General Missionary Committee of the Primitive Methodist connexion and continued to show a deficit to 1875.[42]

Between just under 25 per cent and just over 33 per cent of the total membership of the Boston circuit lived in the town itself in the period 1851 to 1875. Donington circuit was far less concentrated. Between 17 per cent and 18 per cent of its membership in 1853, 1858 — the year in which its numbers reached their highest point — and 1875 belonged to the society based in Donington. The lack of a strong centre was even more marked on the Spalding and Holbeach branch where the membership in rural places such as Holbeach Bank and Little London was more significant than in Spalding and Holbeach, the principal towns of the area. By the late 1860s Whaplode Drove was the most important place in the circuit with a membership of over seventy.[43]

The distribution of membership reflected the success of the Primitive Methodists among the rural workers of the area, but it did not provide a strong enough base on which to support the developing structures of the connexion. This came from the towns which became an increasingly significant element in Primitive Methodist life in south Lincolnshire between 1851 and 1875. These developments also reflected the changing demographic and social structure of the area during the period as the towns grew in relative importance at the expense of the villages.

*   *   *   *   *   *

The maintenance of the connexion's administrative machinery and institutions became a growing preoccupation which threatened other activities. One commentator, writing in the 1880s, argued that 'officialism' was damaging people's spiritual lives and hindering Primitive Methodism's approach to 'the outcasts of society'.[44] The need to provide social activities which were attractive and entertaining enough to bring in money stifled the purely religious life of the chapels. In 1864 the trustees of Spalding and Little London chapels were recommended to reduce the debts on the buildings by holding bazaars.[45] The trustees of Boston West Street chapel arranged a trip to the sea and a tea meeting on the shore in 1866 in aid of its funds.[46] In 1873 Boston circuit committee gave permission for a 'Service of song', to be held two or three times in the winter for chapel renovation funds.[47] Harvest home celebrations and meetings had been held on the Boston circuit since 1865 but by 1867 they were being used to raise money for the circuit's manse furniture fund.[48]

Some events arranged by the chapels had no obvious religious content beyond their endorsement, through speeches and recitations, of morally uplifting sentiments, while their form, with its emphasis on wholesome recreation uncontaminated by rough behaviour and alcohol, was one which was common to many other organisations in the period. In 1860 a correspondent in the *Primitive Methodist Magazine* condemned the 'frivolity and desire for the gratification of the carnal appetite, in pleasure parties, feasts, and trips' which was said to be 'robbing some of our professedly religious people of their religious character'.[49] Boston circuit committee arranged a trip to Barr Sands in August 1865. It was accompanied by bands and refreshments were provided, but no intoxicating drinks were allowed.[50] A harmonium was taken on a boat excursion from Boston to Woodhall Spa arranged by the Boston Primitive Methodists in August 1869 and readings and recitations were given *en route*.[51]

Chapel events were sometimes in danger of being so completely absorbed into the local social calendar that they lost all their distinctive qualities and even developed some which were the antithesis of the values the chapels sought to inculcate. Boston circuit quarterly meeting found it necessary to pass a resolution in 1865 disapproving of 'the system of drinking ale and certain games practised' during the time of Sunday school anniversary services. They also asked that the 'bands of music' should cease to play then. In 1873 the same meeting passed a resolution regretting that:

'proceedings of a questionable character are indulged in at our various school feasts, and hope that steps will be taken by the various school authorities to prevent any irregularities by clearing the fields not later than 7.30 and holding a special religious service'.[52]

The drift towards a position in which Primitive Methodism began to lose the distinctive characteristics which had marked its earlier development was counteracted to some extent by the internal discipline which the connexion exercised over its members and by attempts to renew the spiritual experience of both its members and adherents through religious revival. The connexion's discipline, can be studied from the late 1840s in the circuit records for south Lincolnshire. This helped to shape the lives of individual members by laying down standards of conduct which defined the boundary between those who were inside the connexion and those outside it. It was voluntary and upheld by no other sanctions than those the connexion was able to impose itself, with expulsion as the ultimate penalty. The fact that this discipline could be maintained was an indication of the strength of members' commitment to Primitive Methodism and, by defining areas in which the behaviour of individuals was the concern of the whole connexion, especially in matters which were not always regarded as being worthy of condemnation by those outside it, reinforced their solidarity. It provided security for the individuals who accepted it, giving them firm guidelines for their personal conduct with support from their fellow members who made up the inner core of Primitive Methodism. If any general trend can be discerned in the circuit minute books there was a tendency for the ultimate sanction of expulsion to be used less. However, as late as September 1873 it was noted in the Spalding and Holbeach accounts that a decrease in the local society at Holbeach Bank was due to eight being taken off the books for immorality, one for drunkenness and one for having 'fallen' in a way which was not defined.[53]

As the connexion's local officers worked to maintain discipline in the Primitive Methodist societies of south Lincolnshire they were frequently concerned with areas of conduct which, although not illegal, could affect an individual's personal standing. This meant that many of their decisions defining behaviour which was or was not acceptable for a committed Primitive Methodist appeared to be based on the way an individual's conduct reflected on the connexion. A Brother Hall — Brother was the title given to male Primitive Methodists by their fellow members and females were referred to as Sister, while the title Revd began to be used for ministers by the middle of the nineteenth century — who was insolvent was not allowed to preach on the Donington branch until he had given proof of his disposition to pay his debts, while a Bro. West who belonged to the Boston circuit was to be spoken about reports in September 1857 that he had worked in his garden on Sunday.[54] In 1859 John Holmes was taken off the Donington preaching plan 'for an awful case of lying' while J. Shepherd, also on the Donington circuit, was disciplined by being suspended from all his offices from April to September 1862 for going to a circus and staying at a public house.[55] Some of the young preachers who smoked on their way to appointments in the Boston circuit were to be spoken to in March 1873 'with a view to a discontinuance of such practice'.[56]

Not all the cases which came before Primitive Methodist disciplinary meetings necessarily led to action being taken against the people involved. In 1857 the Grantham quarterly meeting examined the case of Bro. Hand and agreed that he was free from condemnation for keeping a public house for his parents. In September 1861 Bro. Richardson was recommended to be restored as a local preacher in the Spalding and Holbeach branch because his insolvency was occasioned by misfortune and other factors rather than personal failures.[57] Not all offenders were punished, but repetition usually brought disciplinary action on an escalating scale. In September 1858 Bro. Hodgson was forgiven by the Boston circuit authorities for being the worse for liquor, exhorted to be on his guard and to do better in the future. However, in March the next year he was taken off the preachers' plan and suspended from membership for three months for intoxication. In June 1859 he was expelled from the connexion for drunkenness and other unspecified immorality.[58]

Transgressions associated with drink appear frequently in local records. In 1848 the Donington branch suspended a Mr Hearson for getting too much drink and striking John Tebb. George Child, also a member of Donington branch, was 'read out of society' in 1852 for threatening the life of a Christian brother, swearing and drunkenness.[59] Cases of fighting were also dealt with by the local circuit authorities. John English lost his place as a local preacher on the Spalding and Holbeach plan in 1863 for fighting and swearing. In August 1868, Bro. Betts of Whaplode Drove was suspended for quarrelling. A Bro. Stennett not only lost his position as a local preacher but the Spalding and Holbeach authorities also expelled him from the Primitive Methodist society in 1869 for fighting with his neighbour.[60]

Sexual behaviour was another area of personal conduct to which the local Primitive Methodist authorities gave their attention. George Wilson and Esther Northern, who later married, were suspended from membership in the Donington branch for six months until January 1853 for what was described as 'criminal connexion'.[61] In 1860 the Spalding and Holbeach authorities suspended the father of an illegitimate child for three months. The next year Thomas Smith lost both his place as a local preacher and his membership for unspecified immorality.[62]

Connexional discipline might also be applied against people who failed to fulfil their religious obligations as Primitive Methodists. The Boston circuit quarterly meeting agreed in 1859 that a Mrs Rylott should be spoken to about her neglect of Sunday morning worship and her attendance at Wesleyan Sunday school.[63] In 1860 Bro. Everitt of the Donington circuit was reminded that if he continued as a Primitive Methodist he would be expected 'to meet in class &c. according to the discipline of the connexion and also to attend the private means of grace as he may have opportunity.'[64] When G. Hibberd of Benington failed to maintain his financial contributions a note was sent to him by the Boston circuit in 1862 to inform him that 'as he has become too covetous to support Primitive Methodism either with money or effort, he had better go over to Mother Church where they are paid for saying Amen.'[65]

The Primitive Methodist disciplinary code was not entirely concerned with punitive action against wrongdoers, but also attempted to reconcile differences and create harmony within the connexion so that in 1852 the officials of the Donington branch intervened in a quarrel between Bros. Barton and Child. They were 'affectionately urged to settle their quarrel according to the Gospel'.[66]

*   *   *   *   *   *

While the discipline of the connexion helped to define the way of life of the individual Primitive Methodist, the spiritual impetus of the local chapel communities was strengthened by revivalism. The nature of this changed in the course of the nineteenth century as the free-flowing and unpredictable forces of revival on which Primitive Methodism had been built in the 1820s and 1830s became channelled into, and to some extent subordinated to, the established institutions of the connexion. By the second half of the nineteenth century revivalism seemed to bolster up existing patterns rather than sweep large numbers of new converts into Primitive Methodism. Older preoccupations with the devil and his works had not entirely disappeared by 1851 when an account of a revival which began in the Holbeach branch showed the effect of revivalism on local chapel communities. It had:

> been going on, more or less, in various parts of this branch since last July. Several courses of special services have been held, which, under the blessing of Jehovah, have been very effective, and showers of saving grace have been vouchsafed. The consciences of the guilty have been grappled with; a free, full, and present salvation has been urged; and though we have had some dreadful conflicts with the powers of darkness, the hosts of Israel have been more than victorious. Satan's right to the souls of those whom he has long held as his slaves, has been courageously disputed by the servants of the living God; and the grand adversary has, in many cases, been defeated. Jesus has come to our help; the prey has been taken from the mighty; and upwards of 60 souls have professed to obtain the blessing of sin forgiven, and united with the Church of Christ. Persons from the age of fourteen to seventy years are among the saved. Good has been done in every place on the Plan; but Holbeach Bank, Whaplode, Long Sutton, and Gedney Drove End, have specially shared the effects of this glorious visitation of saving power.[67]

The need to work within existing structures meant, however, that revival came to be a planned event. In 1844 revival meetings were held by resolution of the Donington quarterly meeting at Little London, Gosberton Clough and Billingborough. In 1855 the Boston circuit authorities agreed to put prayer meetings on the plan 'at each place a half an hour previous to preaching evening sermon not exceed [*sic*] half an hour and conclude with a prayer meeting for a revival of the word of God'.[68] When Donington circuit authorities resolved 'to employ all the special means we can to bring up the work of God in our circuit' in December 1856 these included the printing of special circulars.[69] Plans for revivals might emanate from local societies, but even in these cases the arrangements were formalised at circuit level. In September 1866 all the local societies on the Spalding and Holbeach mission who had requested revival services were given permission to hold them.[70] In December 1867 Boston circuit quarterly meeting quantified its revival objectives precisely as well as the means that were to be employed to achieve them. It was agreed that there were to be fifteen minutes prayer each day 'for a revival of God's work and we covenant with God and one another for an increase of 50 souls during the next quarter.'[71]

As religious revival developed into a consciously planned operation the Primitive Methodists adopted the American techniques of protracted meetings — consecutive nightly meetings in a chapel lasting for a week or two and sometimes longer with a different preacher or preachers each night — and the employment of revivalists. This was partly as a result of the connexion's contacts with developments in America through its own missions, but the same instruments were also being employed by other evangelical churches for mainly urban missionary work.[72] In 1855 protracted meetings were planned on the Boston circuit at Leake, Boston and Fosdyke, as well as at Stickford, Wainfleet and Wainfleet Bank, Irby and Halton Fen Side in that part of the circuit which extended out of south Lincolnshire. As far as possible travelling preachers were planned to take these.[73]

It is not clear whether the revivalists employed on south Lincolnshire circuits were professionals. In December 1860 a Mrs Sanderson was asked to come 'to assist in holding a few revival services' in the Spalding and Holbeach branch. She was to work 'where the friends may desire to have her'.[74] Boston circuit planned to engage a Mr Corbridge, who was described as 'the revivalist' for a month at the beginning of 1870.[75] The work of these revivalists was clearly designed to strengthen existing institutions rather than transform them. If Mrs Sanderson accepted the invitation of the Spalding and Holbeach branch in 1860 she was to be asked to preach at Holbeach on 16 December 'and make collections for lighting and cleaning'.[76] When the members of Spalding and Holbeach mission were asked to 'pray for an increase of piety' in June 1872 it was with the aim of bringing 'such an increase of members and money that the station may become self-supporting'.[77]

Revival could also arise out of the regular round of services which were the staple of the connexion's religious life, giving them an extra piquancy as well as reaffirming their significance. The annual Sunday school sermons at Long Benington in September 1852 were outwardly conventional in form, but 'the Lord made bare his arm, and two persons professed to find the Lord.'[78] The annual round of special services and public meetings which developed in association with fund raising for missionary work led to a revitalisation of Primitive Methodism in Great Gonerby as well as other places on the Bottesford circuit in 1856. Nearly fifty people were said to have been saved 'among them some of the most profligate' in the village.[79] Missionary services also provided the basis for a revival on Donington circuit in the winter of 1857-8 when members were 'praying that the Lord would pour out his Spirit abundantly upon us'.[80] Their prayers were answered in the new year when 'the converting work' began.[81]

The contrast between the institutionalised revivalism of the second part of the nineteenth century and the earlier phase of Primitive Methodism was also apparent in the reports of camp meetings which in the 1820s and 1830s were symbols of the connexion's commitment to vigorous open air evangelism. They became much more decorous occasions and were an annual event in many places, attended by many people already sympathetic to Primitive Methodism who came for uplift and to reaffirm their established religious position as well as to demonstrate the connexion's strength and unity.[82]

The reports of the 1856 Great Gonerby revival suggest that in this case converts were made from outside the ranks of people usually associated, even marginally, with chapel activities: 'Some of the vilest sinners were rescued from the grasp of the enemy of souls, scoffers were silenced, and many who had previously been hostile to our cause became our friends, and candidly acknowledged that it was indeed the work of God.'[83] Allowance must be made for hyperbole in these statements which need to be seen in the context of the increased importance of institutional-based revivalism in Primitive Methodist life. This meant that potential converts were more likely to come from among those linked in some way with its organisation such as the people who attended services without being members as well as second and third generation Primitives already associated with the connexion by baptism. They were near enough to the chapel and its activities to be touched by the sort of revivalism which worked inside and supported these existing structures.

V

Primitive Methodism in Rural Society

By 1875 the Primitive Methodist connexion had become an accepted part of the lives of the local communities of south Lincolnshire. As this happened it developed common interests with the other Nonconformist churches of the area and a similar approach to other organisations whose aims it often shared such as the temperance and friendly societies. For example, the Primitive Methodist minister joined his Wesleyan, Independent and Baptist counterparts in giving addresses in support of the Grantham Religious Reading Room in 1856.[1] The Boston Primitive Methodists united with the General Baptists, Methodist New Connexion, Wesleyan Methodists and Congregationalists of the town in 1860 for devotional exercises with the aim of promoting a revival.[2] The early support which the Primitives gave to the temperance movement also brought them wider contacts.[3] At the Grantham Temperance Society annual festival in 1857 there were services in the Wesleyan chapel, a public meeting in the Exchange Hall, sermons under the auspices of the Baptists and four week-night lectures in the town's Primitive Methodist chapel.[4]

Many of these developments took place first in the market towns of south Lincolnshire and their spread into the villages was an indication of the way in which Primitive Methodism ceased to draw its real strength and inspiration from its country-based societies and became increasingly dependent on town-based developments. The increase in the importance of the market towns was common to all Methodist bodies as well as being part of a wider movement whereby the countryside was increasingly permeated by urban values and attitudes.[5] Moreover, the towns of south Lincolnshire were themselves intermediaries for organisations based in the larger towns and cities, a process which was helped by the improved communications afforded by the development of Lincolnshire's railway network. Meetings, lectures and similar events could be arranged at which speakers and representatives of national organisations could be present. At another level those families in the villages whose relatives migrated to the towns were brought into contact with urban developments through family relationships.

Primitive Methodist rules sought to keep the connexion in a neutral political position. Its preachers were not allowed to make speeches at parliamentary elections or political meetings. They were employed exclusively for the salvation of souls and interference in politics was beyond their province. As far as individual members were concerned it was felt that 'a Christian ought not to be a turbulent, factious or noisy politician.'[6] The surviving local minute books for the period up to 1875 show that south Lincolnshire Primitive Methodists seem to have generally kept to this neutral political position at an official level. Moreover, their following among labourers and other groups outside the parliamentary electorate meant that the Primitives were a relatively unimportant group in local politics until the franchise was extended in 1884.[7]

However, there are indications that Primitive Methodist ministers and members were beginning to become involved in matters which had political implications and to develop an overtly reformist stance in this respect. As in more exclusively spiritual matters they also began to co-operate with members of other denominations over such matters of general concern as education, temperance and the position of the Church of England. Boston's Nonconformist Association had links with the national anti-religious establishment Liberation Society and was involved in a campaign it conducted in 1860 against church rates.[8] The town continued to be a base for anti-establishment agitation and in 1868 was represented at the triennial conference of the Liberation Society in London.[9] A provisional committee of all the Nonconformist ministers in Grantham was formed in 1873 to support the Association for the Promotion of Religious Equality which in its turn supported Edward Miall's parliamentary campaign for English disestablishment.[10] In 1875 Bourne's Nonconformist ministers appeared together on a platform at a meeting and lecture by a Mr Hastings, the agent of the Liberation Society, although attendance was said to be small.[11]

The issue of education, and especially the election of school boards, brought Nonconformists together in some parts of Lincolnshire in the mid 1870s. At Boston in 1873 they pressed for compulsory school boards as a means of preventing money raised by rates being used for denominational religious education.[12] The

Nonconformists were successful in the 1875 Spalding school board elections in having all their candidates and only one churchman elected — a result which was greeted in the town with great excitement.[13] Attempts to organise labourers' votes at the Bourne elections of 1875 were less successful and the school board there was split between two churchmen and three Nonconformists.[14]

The temperance issue was another reforming platform on which Nonconformists could begin to unite. By the late 1830s the northern-based teetotal movement, which had greater support among dissenters than the more moderate British and Foreign Temperance Society, was growing in importance. It was the teetotallers, advocating total abstinence from intoxicating drinks, who were to feature more prominently in Lincolnshire.[15] They saw themselves as part of a general attack on ignorance, feudalism and rusticity and their followers became caught up in the political implications of this stance. Enthusiasm for industrial progress, science, education and humanitarian movements was implicit in the reports of teetotal meetings in Lincoln in 1839. It was said that the spirit of enquiry resulting from the advance of teetotalism would mean that:

> Man [*sic*] will throw off the yoke of subserviency to the enemies of their species who, under the guise of conservators of the public weal, wheedle their humbler fellow-men to join them in the futile attempt to stem the tide that will inevitably sweep Toryism from the face of the earth. The daylight of truth is dawning, and Mr. Holt and his fellow-labourers are entitled to the hearty gratulations of every liberal politician for their ceaseless endeavours to dispel the mists that becloud the mind; for after all, it is not in the senate, but in the silent homes, in the very bosoms of men, that the great battles for educational, political and religious reforms will be fought and won.[16]

It was suggested in 1839 that there was a connection between teetotalism and Chartism in Boston. A Chartist petition was said to be circulating in the Temperance Hall 'thus converting a moral into a political institution'. Nineteen out of twenty teetotal leaders were said to be rampant Radicals, and among the people who had introduced the petition a man called Mumford was a particularly active temperance advocate. It had been signed by active teetotal leaders and speakers and one was taking it round the town.[17] Similarly, when a Lincoln teetotal anniversary was addressed by a Mr Vincent, probably the Chartist Henry Vincent, it was said that the movement was, 'fast losing all respect, by engaging a list of revolutionary mountebanks who spout the most disgusting falsehoods of their opponents; abuse and insult the Aristocracy, the Church and all our National Institutions, and in fact, substitute political phrenzy for the gin bottle'.[18]

The Primitive Methodists had officially supported the temperance movement from a relatively early date. Their 1832 conference passed a motion approving temperance societies and recommended them to the attention of Primitive Methodists.[19] In 1841 the connexion's General Committee issued a statement that it approved of teetotalism and recommended its prudent advocacy.[20] Until about the middle of the nineteenth century they were, however, enthusiastic consumers of the temperance cause rather than leaders who shaped its development.[21]

The Baptists and Congregationalists were also strong supporters of the temperance movement, but in south Lincolnshire the numerically more significant Wesleyan Methodists were the chief associates of the Primitives in this cause.[22] Grantham's teetotal temperance society was formed at a meeting in the town's Wesleyan chapel in February 1837 — an indication of relatively early interest from this direction.[23] Similarly, a report of teetotal meetings in Lincoln from October 1837 showed that they were being held in a Wesleyan schoolroom.[24] This type of assistance continued at a local level, although it was not until the 1870s that the Wesleyan Methodists began to give official support to the temperance movement.[25] The relatively quick local response of the Wesleyans does not seem to have been affected by the schisms over teetotalism which occurred in other parts of the country.[26] However, the potential for division which existed in Wesleyan Methodism can be seen in Grantham as late as 1870 when a minister declined to give out a notice about a teetotal lecture.[27]

The support of Wesleyan Methodists and other Nonconformist churches on the temperance platform enhanced the movement's standing and, because of their association with them, that of the Primitive Methodists. When a Manchester prohibitionist visited Grantham in 1857 to lecture he first appeared in the Primitive Methodist chapel, then the Wesleyan Reform chapel and the

Exchange Hall.[28] In March the same lecturer spoke five times at the Wesleyan and Primitive chapels in Donington.[29] The Grantham Temperance Society annual festival in 1857 was a further example of inter-denominational co-operation which fully involved the Primitive Methodists.[30]

* * * * * *

The growth of trade unionism among agricultural workers in the 1870s affected the social group from which the Primitive Methodists drew considerable support. The nature and extent of the relationship between the two provides a further illustration of the place which the Primitives had come to occupy in rural society by this period and of their role in it as a movement of reform. In his memoirs Josiah Sage noted that the 'one striking feature' about the leaders of Joseph Arch's union was that most of them were Primitive Methodist local preachers.[31] The theme was taken up by later writers and R.F. Wearmouth commented that:

> Although the Agricultural Trade Unions were ostensibly seeking a material benediction, the religious element was not absent. In motive power and organization, in idea and enthusiasm it was constantly expressed. The influence of Methodism can be seen in these respects. It also provided a discipline and a dynamic.[32]

It has been shown that of 254 men who were active in the Lincolnshire agricultural trade union movement as speakers, chairmen or officials in the period 1872 to 1892, 134 were Methodists. They constituted 99 per cent of those whose religious affiliations were known.[33] Ninety-four of the 254 were from south Lincolnshire and 46 of them had identifiable religious affiliations. All of them, except one Baptist, were Methodists, with 22 Primitives, 10 Free Methodists and 13 Wesleyans.[34]

Union activists who came from among the Primitives employed the rhetorical devices and figures of speech which were used in village chapel pulpits. As well as using biblical imagery union speakers commonly deployed arguments which they based on biblical sources.[35] When George Morris spoke on a Sunday in April 1874 from the steps of the fountain in Bourne market place his subject was the 'Crucifixion of our Lord'. He was said to have preached for an hour, taken a collection on behalf of the locked-out agricultural labourers and announced that he would address them on Monday on the labour question. A report of a meeting at Holbeach St John's in May 1875 referred to 'the Union prophets'.[36]

In some cases the unions adopted the forms of the meetings which were used by the Nonconformist bodies. The Morton branch of the National Agricultural Labourers' Union combined a celebratory harvest home tea and a public meeting in October 1873.[37] A union meeting was held in Gosberton Clough Primitive Methodist chapel in November 1875 when, 'about ninety took tea, after which a public meeting was held; a very good and orderly meeting was opened by singing and prayer; and at the close a collection was made for the funds of the chapel which reached 17s which the members mentioned their intention of making up to a pound.'[38]

In spite of these links the official position of the Primitive Methodist connexion was as unencouraging to trade unionism as it was to other forms of political activity. Fears were expressed that the union movement would disturb the smooth running of chapel affairs. The 1873 annual conference of the connexion noted that trade and agricultural agitations during the past year had led to a decrease in membership in some circuits. Members were urged to maintain their 'Christian Character and deportment, and devotedness to the cause of God'.[39] In December 1875 the Donington circuit authorities passed a resolution advising office holders not to allow 'political or other agitating meetings' to be held in chapels. They wished to avoid 'questions likely to irritate our societies'.[40] In some cases this official policy prevailed and it was reported how a meeting had been arranged at a Primitive Methodist chapel in Long Sutton parish in March 1875 'but some *Christian* brother prevented us from having it, and this is how they are now driving the poor from church and chapel by treating them so harshly.'[41]

However, union meetings were held on Primitive Methodist chapel premises. The schoolroom at Whaplode Drove was used twice for meetings in 1872 at which several working men spoke with 'good feeling and moderation characterised the proceedings'.[42] Similarly, Little London's schoolroom was lent for a union meeting in September 1875, while a meeting at Gosberton Clough chapel later in the same year has already been described.[43]

Nor were the Primitive Methodists the only Nonconformist body to provide the unions with meeting places although chapels, together with the schoolrooms connected with them, only constituted a minority of the places at which union meetings were held. Free Methodist and Wesleyan Reform chapels were also used and at an evening meeting preceded by tea at Whaplode Free Methodist chapel the Revd W. Neal, an active emigration propagandist, spoke on 'Light across the water', Mrs Neal played the harmonium and a collection totalling 14s 6d was taken.[44] The Wesleyan Reform chapel at Wellingore housed a large meeting during a lock-out. It began 'with praise and prayer' and William Banks, the Labour League leader, was the main speaker.[45] The Free Methodists at Sutterton provided accommodation for a union meeting in November 1875.[46] Details of the venues of fifty-eight meetings in south Lincolnshire, other than those held in the open air, were reported in the Labour League's papers the *Labour League Examiner* and the *Labourer* from May 1874 to December 1875. One of these was held in a building used as a chapel and temperance hall, one in a Wesleyan Reform and another in a Wesleyan chapel. The proportion of Nonconformist meeting places used by Joseph Arch's union in south Lincolnshire was slightly higher, but hardly significant. The surviving issues of the *Labourers' Union Chronicle* and the *English Labourer* from June to December 1875 show that the Free Methodist chapels at Sutterton and Whaplode, an unspecified chapel at Sutterton, the Primitive Methodist schoolroom at Gosberton Clough and the Primitive Methodist schoolroom at Little London were the only Nonconformist meeting places used out of the thirty named venues.

The contribution of the Primitive Methodists to the agricultural trade union movement needs therefore to be seen against a background in which official discouragement did not prevent a more positive response in some places at a local level. However the Primitives were not unique in this respect, nor did they provide the movement with a collective political or economic philosophy.[47] It was eclectic and drew its inspiration from a number of the reforming movements, such as the temperance movement, the Liberation Society and the friendly societies, which had reached

the countryside by the 1870s. It was also, like other religious and
reforming movements of the period, strengthened by its
relationship with the towns of the area. Individual leaders such as
William Banks, the Boston stationer, and George W. Bailey of
Spalding, who was at various times a brickmaker, cooper and
mushroom ketchup maker as well as a smallholder, had town-
based occupations. This gave them a degree of independence not
possessed by the agricultural labourer.[48]

Trade union organisation in the towns provided an example to
the agricultural worker as well as some practical and
organisational support. The movement for shorter hours which
reached Lincolnshire by 1871 spread from foundry workers to
other trades in the market towns. In February 1872 Thomas
Vincent of Harlaxton pointed out how the 'success of the
manufacturing and mechanical workpeople' had led the
agricultural labourer to work for 'an advance of wages, and a
shortening of the daily hours of labour'.[49] The Grantham District
United Labourers' Society was active holding meetings in the
villages around the town in the spring of 1872 where the speakers
included labourers from Hornsby's Grantham foundries.[50]
William Earle Welby of Denton Hall maintained that the village
labourers had been 'stirred up by a systematic visitation . . .
carried on by Trades' union delegates'.[51]

Support for the agricultural trade union movement in south
Lincolnshire varied both in terms of where it was most successful
and which branch of the movement found followers in any
particular place. In general terms the unions took root most easily
in the large open villages where the labourers had developed an
independent way of life and where local issues such as the
distribution of parish charities or the question of providing
allotments for labourers could stimulate union activity. The
success of a union in any particular place could also depend on
ideology as well as local leadership. The Labour League led by
William Banks was more closely identified with the nine hours
movement than Joseph Arch's National Union. A slightly greater
proportion of its meetings were held in public houses and club
rooms than those of the Union — possibly an indication that
Banks' organisation might have appealed more to this side of
village life than that led by the Primitive Methodist Joseph Arch.[52]

The varied response to agricultural trade unionism also reflected

Illustrations of Primitive Methodist Chapels with dates of buildings. These illustrations have been arranged in order of building date to provide an indication of the development of styles of chapel architecture in the area.

Gosberton Clough Primitive Methodist Chapel 1835.

Moulton Seas End Primitive Methodist Chapel 1835.

Little Hale Primitive Methodist Chapel 1837.

Little London Primitive Methodist Chapel 1842.

Pinchbeck West Primitive Methodist Chapel 1842.

Claypole Primitive Methodist Chapel 1861.

Holbeach Bank Primitive Methodist Chapel 1864.

Holbeach Primitive Methodist Chapel 1866.

Boston West Street Primitive Methodist Chapel 1866.

Spalding St Thomas's Road Primitive Methodist Chapel 1877.

the way the quality of the relationship between farmers and labourers differed from area to area and from place to place in south Lincolnshire. Small farmers were often closer to the labourer in terms of their economic position and general attitudes than they were to the larger farmers or some of the master tradesmen and craftsmen of the open villages and market towns. They were therefore more likely to be sympathetic to the labourers' aspirations. Where they were more numerous, as in the fens of south Lincolnshire, the local climate was more likely to be sympathetic to the labourers' aspirations.[53] Such a climate would be reflected in the willingness of local chapel leaders to allow the buildings for which they were responsible to be used for union meetings, in spite of official rulings to the contrary.[54]

*   *   *   *   *   *

In the earlier stages of their development in south Lincolnshire, the Primitive Methodists were able, as Ranter revivalists, to provide the rural workers of south Lincolnshire with a means of finding a sense of identity and a degree of emotional security in a period of social change. As the connexion developed, its institutional life became increasingly complex and it began to move into the mainstream of local community life. New priorities emerged as the maintenance of the connexion's institutions was seen to be increasingly important. The prevailing characteristic of the connexion's life became its steady and orderly development as part of local society and it took its place alongside other organisations which sought to bring reform and improvement to the lives of the villagers of south Lincolnshire. The behaviour and attitudes epitomized by Primitive Methodist's Ranter past were not however suddenly jettisoned and many of them continued to be accepted, if only at a superficial level, as part of the connexion's life and heritage to the end of the period under review so that the Primitive Methodist chapel still continued to be seen as a place of worship which rural workers could feel was particularly their own.

Notes

Notes for pages 1-10

Introduction

1. H.B. Kendall, *The Origin and History of the Primitive Methodist Church* 2 vols (London [c.1905]).

2. E.J. Hobsbawm, *Primitive Rebels: studies in archaic forms of social movement in the nineteenth and twentieth centuries* (Manchester, 1971 edn.) 136.

3. Julia Stewart Werner, *The Primitive Methodist Connexion: its background and early history* (Madison, Wisconsin) 74-7.

4. James Obelkevich, *Religion and Rural Society: south Lindsey 1825-1875* (Oxford, 1976) 257; John Munsey Turner, *Conflict and Reconciliation: studies in Methodism and Ecumenism in England 1740-1982* (London, 1985) 86.

5. Hobsbawm, *Primitive Rebels*, 139-41.

I South Lincolnshire 1817-1875

1. Population figures based on census returns published in Parliamentary Papers [subsequently P.P.] 1801-2, VII (9), 206; 1812 XI (316), 191; 1822 XV (502), 187; 1831 XVIII (348), 412; 1843 XXII (496), 158-64, 175; 1852-3 LXXXV (1631), clxxxiv-v; 1862 L (3056), 68; 1872 LXVI - Part I (C.676) vol. 1, 217-18.

2. P.P. 1843 XXII (496), 158-63.

3. P.P. 1862 XVII (2977) 23rd *Annual Report of the Registrar General for Births, Deaths and Marriages*, 296-9; 1872 XVII (C.667) 33rd *Annual Report of the Registrar General for Births, Deaths and Marriages in England*, 336-9.

Notes for pages 10-11

4. P.P. 1863 LIII Part I (3221) *Census* 1861, 129; 1873 LXXI Part I (C.872) *Census* 1871 vol. 3, 386.

5. P.P. 1852-3 LXXXVI (1632) *Population* 1801-51 Division VII, 28-41; LXVI Part II (C.676 - I) *Census* 1871 vol. 2, 347 -53; for the growth of Long Sutton see William White, *History, Gazetteer and Directory of Lincolnshire* . . . (1856 repr. Newton Abbot, 1969) 858-9.

6. J.A. Chartres and G.L. Turnbull, 'Country Craftsmen' in G.E. Mingay (ed.), *The Victorian Countryside*, vol. 1, (London, 1981) 314-15, 317, 327; J.A. Chartres, 'Country Tradesmen', in Mingay (ed.), *Victorian Countryside*, vol. 1, 300-2; P.P. 1852-53 LXXXVIII Part II (1691 - II) *Population* Tables II, 576-83; 1863 LIII Part II (3221) *Census* 1861 Divisions IV to XI, 574-81. Craftsmen have been defined as including millers, brickmakers and dealers, sawyers, cabinet makers, coopers and turners, wheelwrights, blacksmiths, builders, carpenters and joiners, bricklayers, marble masons, masons and paviors, slaters and tilers, plasterers, paperhangers, painters and glaziers, saddlers, tailors and shoemakers. Tradesmen include shopkeepers, butchers, bakers and confectioners, grocers and tea dealers, publicans, beer sellers and innkeepers, ironmongers and drapers.

7. P.P. 1863 LIII Part II (3221) *Census* 1861, Divisions IV to XI, 582-7.

8. P.P. 1867-8 XVII (4048) *Employment of Women and Children in Agriculture*, Appendix, part II, 299; (4068 - I) *Employment of Women and Children in Agriculture*, Appendix, part II, 218, 287.

9. David Grigg, *The Agricultural Revolution in South Lincolnshire* (Cambridge, 1966) 188.

10. H.C. Darby, *The Draining of the Fens* (second edn., 1956, repr. Cambridge, 1968) 144-8; Grigg, *Agricultural*

Notes for pages 11-13

Revolution, 23; T. W. Beastall, *The Agricultural Revolution in Lincolnshire* (Lincoln, 1978) 7.

11. [Arthur Young], *General View of the Agriculture of the County of Lincoln* (second edn., 1813, repr. Newton Abbot, 1970) 255, 261.

12. Ibid., 273.

13. Joan Thirsk, *English Peasant Farming: the agrarian history of Lincolnshire from Tudor to recent times* (London, 1957) 232-4; 314; W.H. Wheeler, *A History of the Fens of South Lincolnshire: being a description of the Rivers Witham and Welland and their estuary, and an account of the reclamation, drainage, and enclosure of the fens adjacent thereto* (second edn., Boston, [1896]) 399, 402-5.

14. Grigg, *Agricultural Revolution*, 66; J.A. Perkins, *Sheep Farming in Eighteenth and Early Nineteenth Century Lincolnshire* (Sleaford, 1977) 9; [James Creasey], *Sketches Illustrative of the Topography and History of New and Old Sleaford, in the county of Lincoln, and of several places in the surrounding neighbourhood* (Sleaford, 1825) 365.

15. Grigg, *Agricultural Revolution*, 50-2, 66, 105; Ph. Pusey, 'On the Agricultural Improvements of Lincolnshire', *Journal of the Royal Agricultural Society of England* (subsequently *J.R.A.S.E.*) 4 (1843) 302.

16. Beastall, *Agricultural Revolution in Lincolnshire*, 173-4; Grigg, *Agricultural Revolution*, 127-9.

17. Pusey, 'Agricultural Improvements of Lincolnshire', 287.

18. Dennis R. Mills, 'Regions of Kesteven devised for purposes of Agricultural History', *Lincolnshire Architectural and Archaeological Society Reports and Papers*, n.s. 7 (1957) 13-15; Grigg, *Agricultural Revolution*, 15 and 100; R.J.

Notes for pages 13-15

Olney, *Lincolnshire Politics 1832-1885* (Oxford, 1973) 28.

19. Grigg, *Agricultural Revolution*, 50, 105-6, 181.

20. Ibid., 16, 79-100; Mills, 'Regions of Kesteven', p. 69; Dennis R. Mills, 'Enclosure in Kesteven', *Agricultural History Review* (subsequently *A.H.R.*) 7, (1959), 84-5.

21. Grigg, *Agricultural Revolution*, 100; Thirsk, *English Peasant Farming*, 301-3; John Algernon Clarke, 'Farming of Lincolnshire', *J.R.A.S.E.* 12 (1851) 376-7.

22. Grigg, *Agricultural Revolution*, 175.

23. Ibid., 155-7, 182-3.

24. W. Marratt, *The History of Lincolnshire: topographical, historical and descriptive*, (Boston, 1814) 84-5; James Saunby Padley, *The Fens and Floods of Mid-Lincolnshire; with a Description of the River Witham in its Neglected State before 1762, and its Improvements up to 1825* (Lincoln, 1882) 39-43; Robert W. Malcolmson, *Popular Recreations in English Society 1700-1850* (Cambridge, 1873) 36-7, 39-40.

25. Dennis R. Mills, 'Population and Settlement in Kesteven (Lincs.), *c.*1775-*c.*1885', (Nottingham Univ. MA, 1957) 63, 79-80, 83; E.A. Wrigley and R.S. Schofield, *The Population History of England 1541-1871: a reconstruction* (London, 1981) 473-5; K.D.M. Snell, *Annals of the Labouring Poor: social change and agrarian England, 1660-1900* (Cambridge, 1985) 180-3.

26. Grigg, *Agricultural Revolution*, 159; Olney, *Lincolnshire Politics*, 53-4.

27. Grigg, *Agricultural Revolution*, 83-4; Olney, *Lincolnshire Politics*, 20.

Notes for pages 15-17

28. D.B. Grigg, 'The Land Tax Returns', *A.H.R.* 11, (1963) 89-90; Grigg, *Agricultural Revolution*, 83-4, 88, 92-3.

29. Grigg, *Agricultural Revolution*, 171.

30. Ibid., 91; Thirsk, *English Peasant Farming*, 264.

31. Grigg, *Agricultural Revolution*, 168-70, 171-2, 175.

32. Ibid., 91-3, 101, 102-3; Olney, *Lincolnshire Politics*, 19-20.

33. Mills, 'Population and Settlement in Kesteven', 39.

34. Mills, 'Regions of Kesteven', 69-75; Thirsk, *English Peasant Farming*, 8; G. Joan Fuller, 'Development of Drainage, Agriculture and Settlement in the Fens of South-East Lincs. during the 19th Century', *East Midland Geographer* 1 (June 1957) 6-7.

35. Beastall, *Agricultural Revolution in Lincolnshire*, 156-9; Clarke, 'Farming of Lincolnshire', *J.R.A.S.E.* 12 (1851) 409; Mills, 'Population and Settlement', 136.

36. P.P. 1867-68 XVII (4068) *Employment of Women and Children in Agriculture*, part I, 73.

37. D.R. Mills, 'The Poor Laws and the Distribution of Population *c.* 1600-1860, with special reference to Lincolnshire', *Transactions and Papers of the Institute of British Geographers* 26 (1959), 189-90; Dorothy M. Owen, *Church and Society in Medieval Lincolnshire* (Lincoln, 1971), 6-10; Mills, 'Population and Settlement in Kesteven', 39.

38. Clarke 'Farming of Lincolnshire', 267.

39. Fuller, 'Development of Drainage, Agriculture and Settlement', 11-12; P.P. 1881 XVI (C.2778 — II)

Notes for pages 17-19

Agricultural Interests. Digest. Appendix to part I of the Evidence, 386, 389.

40. Kenneth Healey, '"Methodism or Nothing. . ." (in Gedney Marsh, 1856)', *Epworth Witness and Journal of the Lincolnshire Methodist History Society* 2, (Autumn 1974) 120; P.P. 1893-94 XXXV (C. 6894 — VI) Royal Commission on Labour *Reports on districts in Lincolnshire*, 12 and 22.

41. M.W. Barley, 'The Lincolnshire Village and its Buildings', *Lincolnshire Historian* 7 (Spring 1951) 257; R.E.G. Cole, *History of the Manor and Township of Doddington, otherwise Doddington-Pigot, in the County of Lincoln . . .*, (Lincoln, 1897) 150.

42. B.A. Holderness, '"Open" and "Close" Parishes in England in the Eighteenth and Nineteenth Centuries', *A.H.R.* 20 (1972), 126-32.

43. White, *Directory of Lincolnshire 1856*, 324-7. 444-7, 471, 547.

44. Dennis Mills, 'English Villages in the Eighteenth and Nineteenth Centuries; a Sociological Approach, part I: the concept of sociological classification', *Amateur Historian* 6 (Summer 1965) 273-5.

45. Village population figures from P.P. 1852-53 LXXXVI (1632) *Population* 1801-51, Division VII, pp. 28-41, 64-6; 1872 LXVI part II (C. 676-I) *Census* 1871 Population Tables vol. 2, 347-53, 365-6.

46. R.J. Olney, *Rural Society and County Government in Nineteenth Century Lincolnshire* (Lincoln, 1979) 77.

47. White, *Directory of Lincolnshire 1856*, 444-5.

48. [Arthur Young], *General View*, (1813), 468.

Notes for pages 19-23

49. White, *Directory of Lincolnshire* (1856) 391; Nikolaus Pevsner and John Harris, *The Buildings of England: Lincolnshire* (Harmondsworth, 1964) 390.

50. *Grantham Journal and Lincolnshire, Leicestershire and Nottinghamshire Advertiser* (subsequently *G.J.*), 9 July 1859.

51. *L.R.S.M.*, 31 Oct. 1856.

52. Lincolnshire Archives Office (subsequently LAO), 2BNL/23/9; Lincolnshire Archives Committee, *Archivists' Report*, 10, 1 Apr. 1958 - 14 Mar. 1959, 18.

53. LAO, 2 ANC 7/14/8.

54. LAO, DIOC MISC 1/10, Notebook of the Revd Samuel Hopkinson, Vicar of Morton with Haconby, 1795-1841. I owe this reference to Dr R.J. Olney.

55. LAO, 3ANC 7/23/23/105.

56. Thirsk, *English Peasant Farming*, 268-9; Beastall, *Agricultural Revolution*, p. 112; S.G. and E.O. Checkland (eds), *The Poor Law Report of 1834*, Penguin edn. (Harmondsworth, 1974) 245.

57. W. Hasbach, *A History of the English Agricultural Labourer* (1908, repr. London, 1966) 268-71.

58. P.P. 1867 XVI (3796) Childrens' Employment Commissioners, *Sixth Report* with Appendix, pp.vii, 7, 28, 33; 1867-8 XVII (4068) *Employment of Women and Children in Agriculture*, 76.

59. Olney, *Rural Society and County Government*, 63-4.

60. 'Condition of the English Peasantry', *Quarterly Review*, 41 (1829) 255, reprinted in C.J. Wrigley (ed.), *The Working*

Notes for pages 23-25

Classes in the Victorian Age Vol. IV: *Rural Conditions 1815-70: debates on the issues from 19th century critical journals* (Farnborough, 1973).

61. John Algernon Clarke, *Fen Sketches, being a Description of the Alluvial District known as the Great Level of the Fens, with a Brief History of its Progressive Improvements in Drainage and Agriculture*, (London, 1852) 263.

62. P.P. 1867-68 XVII (4068) *Employment of Women and Children in Agriculture*, 72-3.

63. *Heckington in the Eighteen Seventies* (Heckington, [1980]) 23.

64. *Drakard's Stamford News and General Advertiser . . .* (subsequently *D.S.N.*), 24 Aug. 1827.

65. *G.J.*, 9 Sept. 1871.

66. P.P. 1852-53 LXXXVIII part II (1691-II) *Population* Tables II, 597; 1862 L (3056) *Census of England and Wales* 1861, 141; 1873 LXXI part II (C.872-I) Population (England and Wales) *General Report*, vol. IV, Appendix A, 127.

67. Grigg, *Agricultural Revolution*, 169.

68. P.P. 1867-68 XVII (4068-I) *Employment of Women and Children in Agriculture*. Appendix part II, 279.

69. *G.J.*, 11 Jan. 1868.

70. P.P. 1867-8 (4068-I), Appendix part II, 282.

71. Jennie Kitteringham, 'Country Work Girls in Nineteenth-century England,' in Raphael Samuel (ed.), *Village Life and Labour* (London, 1975) 111-12.

Notes for pages 25-27

72. P.P. 1843 XII (510) *Employment of Women and Children in Agriculture*, 216.

73. P.P. 1867-68 XVII *Employment of Women and Children in Agriculture*, 86-7; XVII (4068-I) *Employment of Women and Children in Agriculture*, Appendix, part II, 308.

74. Ibid., 299-300.

75. *Spalding Free Press and Eastern Counties Advertiser* (subsequently *S.F.P.*), 16 Oct. 1855.

76. *L.R.S.M.*, 29 May 1857; 10 Aug. 1866.

77. Ibid., 31 Aug. 1849.

78. Olney, *Rural Society and County Government*, 64.

79. P.P. 1865 XXVI (3484) *Seventh Report of the Medical Officer of the Privy Council*, 1864, 135.

80. Olney, *Rural Society and County Government*, 63-4.

81. [Cornelius Greenwood], *A Short Account of the Late Thomas Fawcett, to which is added the Rise and Progress of Methodism in Sleaford* (Sleaford, 1839) 7.

82. [George Oliver], *Scopwickiana; or Sketches and Illustrations of a Secluded Village in Lincolnshire* (Lincoln, 1838) 20.

83. P.P. 1867-68 XVII (4068) *Employment of Women and Children in Agriculture*, 72-3.

Notes for pages 28-29

II Early Primitive Methodism and its Movement into Lincolnshire

1. T. Church, *Sketches of Primitive Methodism* (London, 1847) 8-10; Kendall, *Origin and History*, vol. 1, 42; W.R. Ward, *Religion and Society in England 1790-1850* (London, 1972) 78-82; David Hempton, *Methodism and Politics in British Society 1750-1800* (paperback edn., London 1987) 92-104; W.R. Ward 'The Religion of the People and the Problem of Control, 1790-1830', in C.J. Cuming and Derek Baker (eds), *Popular Belief and Practice: papers read at the ninth summer meeting and the tenth winter meeting of the Ecclesiastical History Society* (Cambridge, 1972) 239-44; Julia Stewart Werner, *The Primitive Methodist Connexion: its background and early history* (Wisconsin, 1984) xi-xii.

2. Richard Carwardine, *Transatlantic Revivalism: popular evangelicalism in Britain and America 1790-1865* (London, 1978) 106; [Lorenzo Dow], *The Dealings of God, Man and the Devil, as Exemplified in the Life, Experience and Travels of Lorenzo Dow* (New York, 1850) 119-20; 123-4.

3. Carwardine, *Transatlantic Revivalism*, 106-7; Kendall, *Origin and History*, vol. 1, 56, 59-61; John Kent, *Holding the Fort: studies in Victorian revivalism* (London, 1978) 44.

4. Kendall, *Origin and History*, vol. 1, 64-5; John T. Wilkinson, *Hugh Bourne 1772-1852* (London, 1952) 47.

5. Kendall, *Origin and History*, vol. 1, 77, 79-82.

6. Wilkinson, *Hugh Bourne*, 69.

7. Kendall, *Origin and History*, vol. 1, 89, 99 and 101.

8. William Antliff, *The Life of Hugh Bourne, Founder of the Primitive Methodist Connexion*, revised by Colin C. McKechnie (London, 1892) 90-1, 93-4.

Notes for pages 29-31

9. Wilkinson, *Hugh Bourne*, 72-3; Antliff, *Hugh Bourne*, 99.

10. Wilkinson, *Hugh Bourne*, 77.

11. Antliff, *Hugh Bourne*, 105.

12. Ibid., 114-17, 119; Wilkinson, *Hugh Bourne*, 84; Werner, *Primitive Methodist Connexion*, 69-70.

13. Kendall, *Origin and History*, vol. 1, 99-106.

14. Wilkinson, *Hugh Bourne*, 86-7, William Garner, *The Life of the Rev. and Venerable William Clowes: one of the patriarchs of the Primitive Methodist Connexion* (London, 1868) 160-1.

15. Kendall, *Origin and History*, vol. 1, 111, 129-32.

16. Wilkinson, *Hugh Bourne*, 87-8; Kendall, *Origin and History*, vol. 1, 113, 132.

17. Werner, *Primitive Methodist Connexion*, 58.

18. Kendall, *Origin and History*, vol. 1, 159.

19. Ibid., 163.

20. Werner, *Primitive Methodist Connexion*, 83; Wilkinson, *Hugh Bourne*, 99.

21. Werner, *Primitive Methodist Connexion*, 83; Kendall, *Origin and History*, vol. 1, 196-7; John Walford, *Memoirs of the Life and Labours of the Late Venerable Hugh Bourne*, vol. 1, (London, 1855) 409-10.

22. Werner, *Primitive Methodist Connexion*, 79.

23. [William Clowes], *The Journals of William Clowes, a*

Notes for pages 31-34

Primitive Methodist Preacher: . . . from the year 1810 to that of 1838 (London, 1844) 116; Kendall, *Origin and History*, vol. 1, 189.

24. H.B. Kendall, 'The Primitive Methodist Church and the Independent Methodist Churches', in W.J. Townsend, H.B. Workman and George Eayrs (eds.), *A New History of Methodism*, vol. 1 (London, 1909) 575.

25. George Herod, *Biographical Sketches of Some of Those Preachers whose Labours Contributed to the Origination and Early Extension of the Primitive Methodist Connexion* (London, n.d.) 300.

26. [Lorenzo Dow], *The Dealings of God, Man and the Devil*, 170-1.

27. Wilkinson, *Hugh Bourne*, 100-1; Kent, *Holding the Fort*, 55-7.

28. Kent, *Holding the Fort*, 56-7.

29. *Lincoln, Rutland and Stamford Mercury* [subsequently *L.R.S.M.*], 25 Sept. 1818.

30. George Herod, *Biographical Sketches*, 188.

31. Ibid.; Garner, 210.

32. A Layman, *Memoir of the Life and Labours of Mr. John Wedgwood* (London, 1870) 31-2, 74.

33. Garner, *William Clowes*, 210.

34. Herod, *Biographical Sketches*, 428-9.

35. Garner, *William Clowes*, 211-12, 214-15.

Notes for pages 34-38

36. Herod, *Biographical Sketches*, 477; Garner, *William Clowes*, 213.

37. Herod, *Biographical Sketches*, 479.

38. *Primitive Methodist Magazine* [subsequently *P.M. Mag.*], 2, (Mar. 1821) 59.

39. Ibid., 2, (Feb. 1821) 45.

40. [Thomas Cooper], *The Life of Thomas Cooper written by himself* (London, 1877) 37-8.

41. John Petty, *The History of the Primitive Methodist Connexion, from its Origin to the Conference of 1860, the First Jubilee Year of the Connexion*, revised and enlarged by James Macpherson (London, 1880) 92.

42. W. Sanderson and W. Harland, *Trophies of Grace or the Power of Religion Manifested* (Hull, 1839) 16-17.

43. Kendall, *Origin and History*, vol. 1, 414.

44. Ibid., 417-19.

45. George Shaw, *The Life of John Oxtoby ('Praying Johnny')* (Hull, 1894) 14-15, 21, 25.

46. Werner, *Primitive Methodist Connexion*, 105-6; Kendall, *Origin and History*, vol. 1, 363-7; Petty, *History*, 85, 87.

47. Petty, *History*, 88.

48. Herod, *Biographical Sketches*, 323, 370.

49. Deborah M. Valenze, *Prophetic Sons and Daughters: female preaching and popular religion in industrial England* (Princeton, 1985) 188-91; Kendall, *Origin and History*,

Notes for pages 38-40

vol. 1, 362-3.

50. Herod, *Biographical Sketches*, 371.

51. Kendall, *Origin and History*, vol. 1, 443-7.

52. William Leary, *Methodist Preaching Plans: a guide to their usefulness to the historian* (Sudbrooke, 1977) illustrations facing pp. 17 and 18.

53. Kendall, *Origin and History*, vol. 1, 449-52.

54. Herod, *Biographical Sketches*, 425; Neil R. Wright, *Lincolnshire Towns and Industry 1700-1914* (Lincoln, 1982) 85, 91.

55. *P.M. Mag.*, 1, (Nov. 1820 for Nov. and Dec. 1819) 257.

56. Clowes, *Journals*, 142; Herod, *Biographical Sketches, 419;* John Davison, *The Life of the Venerable William Clowes: one of the founders of the Primitive Methodist Connexion* (London, 1854) 96-7; Garner, *William Clowes*, 218-19.

57. John T. Wilkinson, *William Clowes 1780-1851* (London, 1951) 42.

58. *L.R.S.M.*, 4 Dec. 1818.

59. Ibid., 28 May 1819.

60. *L.R.S.M.*, 9 July 1819; *P.M. Mag.* n. s. 10, (May 1840) 181.

61. *L.R.S.M.*, 16 July 1819.

62. *P.M. Mag.*, n. s. 10, (May 1840) 181; Kendall, *Origin and History*, vol. 1, 464.

63. Herod, *Biographical Sketches*, 362.

Notes for pages 40-42

64. Ibid., 364.

65. Ibid., 364-5.

66. *P.M. Mag.*, 2, (Mar. 1821) 57; Herod, *Biographical Sketches*, 303.

67. *P.M. Mag.*, 2, (Mar. 1821) 57-8.

68. Ibid. (Feb. 1821) 45-6; Kendall, *Origin and History*, vol. 1, 462-3.

69. Ibid., 45-6.

70. Ibid., (Mar. 1821) 58-60.

71. Ibid.

72. Ibid., 60.

73. Ibid., (Feb. 1821) 31; Herod, *Biographical Sketches*, 364.

74. *P.M. Mag.*, 2, (Feb. 1821) 32.

75. Ibid., n. s. 12, (Oct. 1842) 314; n. s. 10 (Jan. 1840) 6-7.

76. Ibid., n. s. 10, (May 1840) 142.

77. Ibid., 11, third ser. (Mar. 1851) 189.

78. Ibid., 2, (June 1821) 131.

79. 'General Minutes of Meetings held by the Primitive Methodist Connexion, Halifax, 1821', p.16 in Robert Smith (ed.), *Minutary Records: being rules, regulations and reports, made and published by the Primitive Methodist Connexion*, I, 1814-30 (Leeds, 1854).

Notes for pages 43-44

80. *P. M. Mag.*, 3, (Apr. 1822) 94; Petty, *History*, 158; *L.R.S.M.*, 7 Dec. 1821.

81. *P. M. Mag.*, 3, (Apr. 1822) 94; *L.R.S.M.*, 22 June 1821.

82. Petty, *History*, 158, referring to Fieldsend's journal.

83. Ibid., 149.

84. Lincolnshire Library Service, Local Studies Collection, Lincoln Reference Library, Broadsheet 946, *Lincoln Circuit. The Lord's Day Plan of the Preachers called Primitive Methodists: known also by the name of Ranters* (1821); for Timberland see above p.42.

85. Ibid.; 'General Minutes . . . 1821', 16; '1822 General Minutes . . . ', p.19 in Smith (ed.), *Minutary Records*, I, 1814-30; General Consolidated Minutes of the Primitive Methodist Connexion approved by the 30th Annual Conference, Sunderland, 1849 (London, 1850) 28-30.

86. 'Minutes of a Meeting held at Nottingham . . . 1819 . . . ', p.11 in Smith (ed.), *Minutary Records*, I, 1814-30.

87. 'General Minutes . . . ', pp.17, 19 and 'Primitive Methodist Connexion Minutes . . . 1823, Leeds', p.7 in Smith (ed.), *Minutary Records*, I, 1814-30. Membership statistics are based on the figures given in Smith (ed.), *Minutary Records*, I-VII, 1814-70 (Leeds, 1852, 1854 and 1863, Burnley, 1853, Bradford, 1866, London, 1871) and J. Ayrton (ed.), *Minutary Records*, VIII, 1871-75 (Horbury, 1882) supplemented by material from Journals of Conference or Annual Meeting 1827-75 [John Rylands University Library of Manchester, Methodist Archives, Primitive Methodist Connexion, MAW MS 730-36] and the *Primitive Methodist Magazine*.

88. *L.R.S.M.*, 21 June 1822.

Notes for pages 44-47

89. 'Large Minutes of the Primitive Methodist Connexion, 1824', p.33 in Smith (ed.), *Minutary Records*, I, 1814-30.

90. *P. M. Mag.*, 4, Nov. 1823, 252; '1822 General Minutes . . . ', p. 19 in Smith (ed.), *Minutary Records*, I, 1814-30; Kendall, *Origin and History*, vol. 1, 262.

91. Kendall, *Origin and History*, vol. 1, 434.

92. Petty, *History*, 251.

93. Herod, *Biographical Sketches*, 429; Petty, *History*, 250-1.

94. *P. M. Mag.*, 9, (Apr. 1828) 141; 11, third ser. (Mar. 1851) 189.

III   Ranter Preaching

1. Letter on Ranters, *Christian Remembrancer*, 3, (Mar. 1821) 130-7.

2. John Gair, 'Rev. John Dickenson', in W. J. Brownson, J. Gair, T. Mitchell and D. S. Prosser (ed.), *Heroic Men: the death roll of the Primitive Methodist ministry, being sketches of those ministers who have died between the conferences of 1888-9* . . . (London, [1889]) 133-5.

3. Shaw, *John Oxtoby*, 41, 43 and 49.

4. Harvey Leigh, *"Praying Johnny"; or, the Life and Labours of John Oxtoby Primitive Methodist Minister* (sixth edn., London, 1867) 80-2.

5. Z. Taft, *Biographical Sketches of the Lives and Public Ministry of Various Holy Women* . . . vol. 2 (Leeds, 1828) 198-9; 288, 290; Herod, *Biographical Sketches*, pp. 324, 364-5, 370-4; Valenze, *Prophetic Sons and Daughters*, 37, 47,

Notes for pages 47-50

108-9, 121, 187-90.

6. *P. M. Mag.*, 9, (Aug. 1828) 257-8.

7. Ibid., n.s. 8, (May 1870) 300; Valenze, *Prophetic Sons and Daughters*, 22-3.

8. *L.R.S.M.*, 28 May 1819; 20 Aug. 1819.

9. Ibid., 28 May 1819.

10. Ibid., 16 June 1820.

11. Werner, *The Primitive Methodist Connexion*, 58.

12. Letter on Ranter Meetings, *Christian Remembrancer*, 1, (Aug. 1819) 469.

13. *P. M. Mag.*, 3, (Jan. 1822) 17-18.

14. Ibid.

15. Ibid., 1, (Nov. 1820) 257; ibid., n.s. 2, July 1831) 248; third ser., 1, (June 1843) 205.

16. Ibid., 9, (Sept. 1828) 314-15.

17. Ibid., n.s. 9, (Apr. 1839) 131.

18. Ibid., 9, (Sept. 1828) 314-15.

19. Thomas Church, *Gospel Victories; or missionary anecdotes of imprisonments, labours and persecutions, endured by Primitive Methodist preachers between the years 1812 and 1842* (London, 1851) 16-17.

20. John Walsh, 'Methodism and the Mob in the Eighteenth Century', in G. J. Cuming and Derek Baker (ed.), *Popular*

Notes for pages 50-53

Belief and Practice: papers read at the ninth summer meeting and tenth winter meeting of the Ecclesiastical History Society (Cambridge, 1972) 213.

21. *P. M. Mag.*, 2, (Feb. 1821) 45.

22. Richard Heath, *The English Via Dolorosa or Glimpses of the History of the Agricultural Labourer* (London, 1884) 63.

23. Mrs Gutch and Mabel Peacock, *Examples of Printed Folk-Lore Concerning Lincolnshire* (repr. Liechtenstein, 1967) 57; Obelkevich, *Religion and Rural Society*, 259-63.

24. Gutch and Peacock, *Folk-Lore Concerning Lincolnshire*, 57; Obelkevich, *Religion and Rural Society*, 262.

25. Obelkevich, *Religion and Rural Society*, 328-9.

26. Kendall, *Origin and History*, vol. 1, 147.

27. Wilkinson, *Hugh Bourne*, 1, 72, 80; Walford, *Hugh Bourne*, 158; Herod, *Biographical Sketches*, 270; Kendall, *Origin and History*, 1, 148-50.

28. 'The Church in Lincolnshire', *Union Review*, 3 (1865) 269.

29. Obelkevich, *Religion and Rural Society*, 276-9.

30. M. G. W. Peacock, 'Folklore and Legends of Lincolnshire', unpublished typescript, Folklore Society Library, University College, London, FLS B70 PEA, 195-6, 212, 286; Augustus Jessop, *Arcady: for better for worse* (London, 1887) 72-82.

31. *P. M. Mag.*, 9, (Aug. 1828) 258-9.

32. Ibid., 260.

33. Ibid., n.s. 5, (Oct. 1835) 390; 1, third ser. (Aug. 1843) 320.

Notes for pages 53-56

34. Ibid., 7, third ser. (Oct. 1849) 579.

35. Ibid., 1, (July 1819) 191-2.

36. J. R. Parkinson, 'The Church Below and the Church Above', in Anon, ed., *The Primitive Pulpit, being Original Sermons and Sketches by Various Ministers of the Primitive Methodist Connexion*, 1, (London, 1857) 187.

37. *P. M. Mag.*, 2, (Feb. 1821) 32.

38. Ibid., 9, (Apr. 1828) 142.

39. Ibid., n.s. 5, (Jan. 1867) 48.

40. Ibid., 17, third ser. (Sept. 1859) 516-17.

41. Ibid., n.s. 9, (Jan. 1839) 11.

42. J. R. Parkinson, 'The Church Below and the Church Above', *The Primitive Pulpit*, 1, 188.

43. Thomas Lowe (ed.), *Burning Words; or, Choice Remains of the late Rev. Robert Key, of Norfolk* (Barnsley, 1882) 13-15.

44. Parkinson Milson, 'Holiness Essential to Seeing the Lord', *The Primitive Pulpit*, 1, 342-3.

IV Chapel Life

1. LAO Parts of Kesteven, Clerk of the Peace's Papers, 'A Return of the Number of Places of Worship not of the Church of England, June 1829' published by R. W. Ambler in *Lincolnshire History and Archaeology*, 20 (1985) 59-64 as 'Religious Life in Kesteven - A Return of the Number of Places of Worship not of the Church of England'. The returns did not include the boroughs of Grantham and

Notes for pages 56-60

Stamford as well as twelve places in the soke of Grantham and four villages to the south of Lincoln which were part of the administrative county of the city.

2. Public Record Office (subsequently PRO), HO 129/442/5/12/23.

3. *G.J.*, 12 June 1858.

4. Ibid., 24 Sept. 1870.

5. PRO, HO 129/175, 421-8, 442. The returns of the 1851 Census of Religious Worship for Lincolnshire have been published [R. W. Ambler (ed.), *Lincolnshire Returns of the Census of Religious Worship 1851*, Lincoln Record Society, 72 (1979)].

6. *P. M. Mag.*, n.s. 5, (May 1835) 189.

7. Ibid., n.s. 6, (Sept. 1836) 346-7.

8. Ibid., n.s. 5, (Oct. 1835) 392-3.

9. Ibid., n.s. 7, (Dec. 1837) 472-3.

10. *P. M. Mag.*, n.s. 5, (Oct. 1835) 392.

11. White, *Directory of Lincolnshire*, 1856, 323; *P. M. Mag.*, n.s. 9, (Dec. 1839) 459.

12. PRO, HO 129/175, 421-8, 442.

13. LAO, Meth B/Boston Primitive Methodist Connexion Quarter Day Accounts 1851-75; Spalding Gentlemen's Society [subsequently S.G.S.], Methodist Archives, Primitive Methodist Church, Wisbech Circuit Accounts 1845-49, Holbeach Branch, Accounts and Membership List 1849-54; Obelkevich, *Religion and Rural Society*, 241.

Notes for pages 60-63

14. P. P. 1852-53 LXXXIX (1690) *Religious Worship* 1851, cclxxxix.

15. Attendances for south Lincolnshire calculated from PRO, HO 129/175, 421-8, 442.

16. PRO, HO 129/425/2/6/11 and 129/431/1/2/2.

17. Ibid., HO 129/428/1/17/32.

18. Henry Pelling, *Politics and Society in Late Victorian Britain* (London, 1968) 22-5; see for example the comments of the Rector of Swaby (PRO, HO 129/431/1/2/2).

19. PRO, RG 4/1645, Non Parochial Registers, Lincoln Primitive Methodist Baptismal Register 1823-37; LAO, Meth B/Lincoln North Circuit /33/ Register of Baptisms 1/ Lincoln Primitive Methodist Circuit 1842-73; Ibid., 2/Lincoln 2nd Primitive Methodist Circuit, 1870-1904, 1873-1911; PRO, RG 4/1930 Boston Primitive Methodist Baptismal Register, 1823-37; LAO, Meth B/Boston Circuit /33/1/ Register of Baptisms 1844-89; SGS, Methodist Archives, Primitive Methodist Church, Baptismal Register for Spalding, Little London, and other chapels 9 May 1844 -26 June 1881, Baptismal Register Donington Circuit 24 Dec. 1843 - 10 Dec. 1893; LAO, Meth B/Sleaford Circuit /45/ Register of Baptisms 1850-65; Ibid., 33/1/ Register of Baptisms 1865-94.

20. Obelkevich, *Religion and Rural Society*, 240-1. For customs surrounding baptism see for example Gutch and Peacock, *Lincolnshire Folk-Lore*, 228-9.

21. Kenneth Healey, ' "Methodism or Nothing . . ."', 120-2.

22. LAO, Cor B5/4/54/1.

23. Boston Centenary Methodist Church, Circuit Chapel Deeds,

Notes for pages 63-66

Packet Nos. 3, 31 and 33, Fosdyke (1826 and 1874), Hubberts Bridge (1871); Spalding Methodist Church, Circuit Chapel Deeds, Moulton Seas End (1835 and 1854), Little London (1842 and 1866), Pinchbeck West (1842 and 1873), Weston Hills (1853), Bicker (1834), Spalding (1870); Sleaford Northgate Methodist Church, Circuit Chapel Deeds, Little Hale (1836 and 1875), Helpringham (1840 and 1848), Ancaster (1843).

24. P.P. 1867-68 XVII (4068) *Employment of Women and Children in Agriculture*, part I, 74.

25. *G. J.*, 17 Oct. 1857.

26. Ibid., 27 Feb. 1858.

27. Ibid., 6 Mar. 1858.

28. Ibid.

29. Ibid., 7 July 1860; for subsequent annual services see 6 July 1861; 5 July 1862; 2 July 1864; 7 July 1866.

30. Ibid., 11 May 1861; 29 Apr. 1865.

31. Ibid., 7 Apr. 1866.

32. Ibid., 10 May 1863; 2 Apr. 1864.

33. Ibid., 19 Apr. 1873; 18 Oct. 1873; 8 Nov. 1873; 22 Nov. 1873.

34. Ibid., 31 Dec. 1870.

35. Sleaford Northgate Methodist Church, Circuit Chapel Deeds, Little Hale.

36. LAO, Meth B/Boston Circuit/55/1/Correspondence File 1861-94.

Notes for pages 66-69

37. Ibid.

38. Sleaford Northgate Methodist Circuit, Chapel Deeds, Ancaster and Helpringham.

39. LAO, Meth C/Boston, West Street Primitive Methodist (Boston Circuit)/24/1/Trust Minutes 1866-74, 31 Jan. 1866.

40. Ibid., /25/1/Trust Minutes 1839-62, note in front of minute book.

41. Ibid., Meth B/Boston Circuit/42/1 and 2/ Quarter Day Accounts 1851-74 and 1874-92; SGS, Methodist Archives, Primitive Methodist Church, Donington Circuit Account Book 1853-78.

42. SGS, Methodist Archives, Primitive Methodist Church, Account of the Moneys and Members in the Spalding and Holbeach Branch of the Donington Circuit 1857-62 and the Spalding and Holbeach Mission 1862-78.

43. LAO, Meth B/Boston Circuit /42/1 and 2/ Quarter Day Accounts 1851-74 and 1874-92; SGS, Methodist Archives, Primitive Methodist Church, Donington Circuit Account Book 1853-78; An Account of the Moneys and Members in the Spalding and Holbeach Branch of Donington Circuit 1857-62, and the Spalding and Holbeach Mission 1862-78.

44. An Old Fashioned Methodist [George Walker], *Methodist Ritualism, or a Few Thoughts on the Methodism of To-day* (London, [1885]) 39-40.

45. SGS, Methodist Archives, Primitive Methodist Church, Spalding and Holbeach Mission Quarterly Meeting Minute Book 1862-83, 6 Dec. 1864.

46. LAO, Meth C/Boston, West Street (Boston Circuit)/24/1/ Trust Minutes 1866-74, June 1866.

Notes for pages 69-71

47. Ibid., Meth B/Boston Circuit/49/2/ Circuit Committee Minutes 1869-87, 17 Sept. 1873.

48. Ibid., 41/1/ Quarterly Meeting Minutes 1855-1867, 12 June 1865; 26 Aug. 1867.

49. *P. M. Mag.*, 18, third ser. (Sept. 1860) 536.

50. LAO, Meth. B/Boston Circuit /41/1/Quarterly Meeting Minutes 1855-67, 2 Aug. 1865.

51. Ibid., 49/2/ Circuit Committee Minutes 1869-87, 30 July 1869.

52. Ibid., 41/1/ Quarterly Meeting Minutes 1855-67, 12 June 1865; 41/3/ Quarterly Meeting Minutes 1869-83, 10 Mar. 1873.

53. SGS, Methodist Archives, Primitive Methodist Church, Account of the Moneys and Members in the Spalding and Holbeach Branch of the Donington Circuit 1857-62, and the Spalding and Holbeach Mission 1862-78.

54. Ibid., Donington Branch Minute Book 1834-55, 2 Mar. 1849; LAO, Meth B/Boston Circuit /41/1/ Quarterly Meeting Minutes 1855-67, 14 Sept. 1857.

55. SGS, Methodist Archives, Primitive Methodist Church, Donington Quarterly Meeting Minute Book 1856-73, 20 June 1859; 24 Apr., 15 Sept. 1862.

56. LAO, Meth B/Boston Circuit /41/3/ Quarterly Meeting Minutes 1869-83, 10 Mar. 1873.

57. Ibid., Grantham /41/1/ Grantham Primitive Methodist Quarterly Meeting Minutes 1855-66, 14 Sept. 1857; SGS, Methodist Archives, Primitive Methodist Church, Donington Circuit, Spalding and Holbeach Branch Quarterly Meeting

Notes for pages 71-74

1860-2, 9 Sept. 1861.

58. LAO, Meth B/Boston Circuit /41/1/ Circuit Quarterly Meeting Minutes 1855-67, 13 Sept. 1858; 14 Mar. 1859; 13 June 1859.

59. SGS, Methodist Archives, Primitive Methodist Church, Donington Branch Minute Book 1834-55, 25 Feb. 1848; 15 Aug. 1852.

60. Ibid., Spalding and Holbeach Mission Quarterly Meeting Minute Book 1862-83, 7 Dec. 1863; 31 Aug. 1868; 3 June 1869.

61. Ibid., Donington Branch Minute Book 1834-55, 30 July 1852.

62. Ibid., Donington Circuit, Spalding and Holbeach Quarterly Meeting 1860-2, 18 Apr. 1860; 11 Mar. 1861.

63. LAO, Meth B/Boston Circuit /41/1/ Quarterly Meeting Minutes 1855-67, 13 June 1859.

64. SGS, Methodist Archives, Primitive Methodist Church, Donington Quarterly Meeting Minute Book 1856-73, 18 Dec. 1860.

65. LAO, Meth B/Boston Circuit /41/1/ Quarterly Meeting Minutes 1855-67, 17 June 1862.

66. SGS, Methodist Archives, Primitive Methodist Church, Donington Branch Minute Book 1834-55, 9 Aug. 1852.

67. *P. M. Mag.*, 10, third ser. (Apr. 1852) 239.

68. SGS, Methodist Archives, Primitive Methodist Church, Donington Branch Minute Book 1834-55, 9 Sept. 1844; LAO, Meth B/Boston Circuit /41/1/ Minutes 1855-67, 10 Dec. 1855.

Notes for pages 74-75

69. SGS, Methodist Archives, Primitive Methodist Church, Donington Quarterly Meeting Minute Book 1856-73, 29 Dec. 1856.

70. Ibid., Spalding and Holbeach Mission, Quarterly Meeting Minute Book 1862-83, 3 Sept. 1866.

71. LAO, Meth B/Boston Circuit /41/2/ Quarterly Meeting Minutes 1867-9, 9 Dec. 1867.

72. Richard Carwardine, *Transatlantic Revivalism*, 107, 198; Obelkevich, *Religion and Rural Society*, 226.

73. LAO, Meth B/Boston Circuit /41/1/ Quarterly Meeting Minutes 1855-67, 10 Dec. 1855.

74. SGS, Methodist Archives, Primitive Methodist Church, Donington Circuit, Spalding and Holbeach Branch Quarterly Meeting 1860-2, 6 Dec. 1860.

75. LAO, Meth B/Boston Circuit /41/3/ Quarterly Meeting Minutes 1869-83, 14 June 1869.

76. SGS, Methodist Archives, Primitive Methodist Church, Donington Circuit, Spalding and Holbeach Branch Quarterly Meeting 1860-2, 6 Dec. 1860.

77. Ibid., 1862-83, 3 June 1872.

78. *P. M. Mag.*, 10, third ser. (Dec. 1852) 739-40.

79. Ibid., 14, third ser. (May 1856) 308.

80. Ibid., 16, third ser. (Feb. 1858) 107-8 and 112.

81. Ibid., (Mar. 1858) 177.

82. *Sleaford Gazette and South Lincolnshire Advertiser*,

Notes for pages 75-78

12 June 1875.

83. *P. M. Mag.*, 16, third ser. (June 1858) 364.

V   Primitive Methodism in Rural Society

1. *G. J.*, 23 Feb. 1856.

2. *Boston Guardian and Lincolnshire Advertiser* [subsequently *B.G.*], 21 Jan. 1860.

3. Kendall, *Origin and History*, vol. 1, 471-2; Brian Harrison, *Drink and the Victorians: the temperance question in England 1815-72* (London, 1971) 179.

4. *G. J.*, 18 Apr. 1857.

5. Alan Rogers, 'When City speaks for County: the emergence of the town as a focus for religious activity in the nineteenth century', in Derek Baker (ed.), *The Church in Town and Countryside: papers read at the seventeenth summer meeting and eighteenth winter meeting of the Ecclesiastical History Society* (Oxford, 1979) 336, 339-41.

6. Thomas Church, *Sketches of Primitive Methodism*, 53.

7. R. J. Olney, *Lincolnshire Politics*, 64; R. C. K. Ensor, *England 1870-1914* (repr. Oxford, 1960) 88; John Vincent, *The Formation of the British Liberal Party 1857-1868*, (Penguin edn., Harmondsworth, 1972) 22; for the size of the south Lincolnshire electorate see Olney, *Lincolnshire Politics*, 255-7.

8. *B. G.*, 10 Mar. 1860; G. I. T. Machin, *Politics and the Churches in Great Britain 1832 to 1868* (Oxford, 1977) 306-7.

9. *B. G.*, 2 Mar. 1867; 2 May 1868.

Notes for pages 78-80

10. *G. J.*, 22 Mar. 1873; Edward Norman, *Church and Society in England 1770-1970: a historical study* (Oxford, 1976) 191.

11. *G. J.*, 6 Mar. 1875.

12. *B. G.*, 21 June 1873.

13. *S. F. P.*, 9 Nov. 1875.

14. *G. J.*, 12 Dec. 1874; 19 Dec. 1874; 2 Jan. 1875.

15. Brian Harrison, *Drink and the Victorians: the temperance question in England 1815-72* (London, 1971) 108-9.

16. *L. R. S. M.*, 1 Nov. 1839.

17. *Boston, Lincoln, Louth and Spalding Herald*, 26 Mar. 1839; 16 Apr. 1839.

18. Brian Harrison, *Drink and the Victorians*, 387; *Boston, Stamford, and Lincolnshire Herald*, 10 Apr. 1849.

19. Kendall, *Origin and History*, vol. 1, 470-2.

20. Ibid., 472.

21. Harrison, *Drink and the Victorians*, 179.

22. Kendall, *Origin and History*, vol. 1, 476.

23. *L. R. S. M.*, 3 Feb. 1837.

24. *L. R. S. M.*, 13 Oct. 1837.

25. R. Waddy Moss, 'Wesleyan Methodism - The Last Fifty Years' in W. J. Townsend, H. B. Workman and George Eayrs (eds.), *A New History of Methodism*, vol. 1 (London, 1909) 465; Frank Baker, *A Charge to Keep: an introduction*

Notes for pages 80-82

to the people called Methodists (repr. London, 1954).

26. Owen Chadwick, *The Victorian Church*, pt. 1 (London, 1966) 378.

27. *G. J.*, 16 Apr. 1870.

28. *G. J.*, 3 Jan. 1857.

29. *B. G.*, 18 Mar. 1857.

30. *G. J.*, 18 Apr. 1857.

31. Josiah Sage, *The Memoirs of Josiah Sage: concerning Joseph Arch and the pioneering days of trade unionism among the agricultural workers* (London, 1951) 48.

32. Robert F. Wearmouth, *Methodism and the Working-Class Movements of England 1800-1850* (London, 1937) 270.

33. Nigel Scotland, *Methodism and the Revolt of the Field: a study of the Methodist contribution to agricultural trade unionism in East Anglia 1872-96* (Gloucester, 1981) 58.

34. Ibid., 88-93, 195-8, 200-1.

35. Ibid., 89 and 147.

36. *G. J.*, 18 Apr. 1874; *Labourers' Union Chronicle* [subsequently *L.U.C.*], 12 June 1875.

37. *L. U. C.*, 11 Oct. 1873.

38. *English Labourer* [subsequently *E. L.*], 27 Nov. 1875.

39. 'Minutes made at the Fifty-Fourth Annual Conference of the Primitive Methodist Connexion . . . London . . . 1873', p.88 in J. Ayrton (ed.), *Minutary Records*, VIII, 1871-5

Notes for pages 82-84

(Horbury, 1882).

40. SGS, Methodist Archives, Primitive Methodist Church, Donington Circuit Quarterly Meeting Minute Book 1873-97, 6 Dec. 1875.

41. *Labourer*, [subsequently *L.*], 27 Mar. 1875.

42. *S. F. P.*, 12 Mar. and 2 Apr. 1872.

43. *E. L.*, 25 Sept. 1875; 27 Nov. 1875 and above p.82.

44. *L. U. C.*, 9 Jan. 1875; for Neal's activities in connection with emigration see, for example *S. F. P.*, 20 and 27 Oct. 1874.

45. *L.*, 17 Apr. 1875.

46. *E. L.*, 27 Nov. 1875.

47. E. J. Hobsbawm, *Primitive Rebels: studies in archaic forms of social movements in the 19th and 20th centuries* (1959, repr. Manchester, 1971) 139.

48. J. P. D. Dunbabin (ed.), *Rural Discontent in Nineteenth Century Britain*, (London, 1974), 74; R. J. Olney, *Rural Society and County Government in Nineteenth Century Lincolnshire* (Lincoln, 1979) 86; Scotland, *Methodism and the Revolt of the Field*, 188, 192, 195.

49. Olney, *Rural Society and County Government*, 88-9; *G. J.*, 2 Mar. 1872.

50. *G. J.*, 23 Mar. 1872; 30 Mar. 1872.

51. Ibid., 13 Apr. 1873.

52. Olney, *Rural Society and County Government*, 89-90.

Notes for page 85

53. Wheeler, *A History of the Fens of South Lincolnshire*, 414; P.P. 1867-68 XVII (4068) *Employment of Women and Children in Agriculture*, 74.

54. See above pp.82-3.

Bibliography

Manuscript Sources

The dates shown relate to the period for which these collections were consulted.

1. *National Collections*

   John Rylands University Library of Manchester.
   Methodist Archives, Primitive Methodist Connexion, Journals of Conference or Annual Meeting, MAW MS 730-36 (1827-75).

   P.R.O., London
   Non-Parochial Registers R. G. 4/1645 & 1930 (1823-37).
   Returns of the 1851 Census of Religious Worship, H.O.129/175, 421-8, 442.

2. *Lincolnshire Archives Office, The Castle, Lincoln.*

   Ancaster Deposit, ANC (1818-68).
   Brownlow Deposit, BNL (1810-51).
   Correspondence of Bishop Kaye, Cor B5/4 (1827-53).
   Fane Deposit, FANE (1805-75).
   Jarvis Deposit, JARVIS (1811-75).
   Lincoln Diocesan Records, Notebook of the Revd Samuel Hopkinson, Vicar of Morton with Haconby, DIOC MISC 1/10 (1795-1841).
   Methodist Records, METH (1835-75).
   Parts of Kesteven, Clerk of the Peace's Papers,
   Return of the Number of Places of Worship not of the Church of England (June 1829).

3. *Records in Other Custody*

   Boston Centenary Methodist Church, Circuit Chapel Deeds (1826-74).

Humberside Libraries and Arts, Grimsby Central Library, copy of Thomas Ogden's manuscript 'A Few of the Persons I have known', R801: 920 0GD (1835-75).
Sleaford Northgate Methodist Church, Sleaford Methodist Circuit Chapel Deeds (1836-75).
Spalding Gentlemen's Society, Methodist Archives (1834-75).
Spalding Methodist Church, Circuit Chapel Deeds (1834-73).

Theses and Other Unpublished Typescripts

Ambler, R. W., 'Social Change and Religious Experience: aspects of rural society in south Lincolnshire with specific reference to Primitive Methodism, 1815-1875' (Hull University Ph.D., 1984).

Mills, Dennis R., 'Population and Settlement in Kesteven (Lincs.), *c.* 1775 - *c.* 1885' (Nottingham University M.A., 1957).

Peacock, M. G. W., 'Folklore and Legends of Lincolnshire', unpublished typescript, Folklore Society Library, University College, London, FLS B70 PEA.

Printed Sources

1. *Newspaper and Periodical Literature*

a) **Local**

Boston Guardian and Lincolnshire Advertiser later: *Boston and Louth Guardian and Lincolnshire Advertiser; Boston, Lincoln and Louth Guardian, and Lincolnshire Advertiser; Lincolnshire Guardian; Lincolnshire Guardian and News; Boston Guardian; Boston Guardian and Lincolnshire News; Boston Guardian and Lincolnshire Independent.*

Boston, Lincoln and Louth Herald and County Advertiser later *Boston, Lincoln, Louth and Spalding Herald.*

Boston, Stamford and Lincolnshire Herald.

Drakard's Stamford News and General Advertiser for the Counties of Lincoln, Rutland, Northampton, Huntingdon, Cambridge, Leicester, Nottingham and Parts Adjacent.

Grantham Journal and Lincolnshire, Leicestershire and Nottinghamshire Advertiser later: *Grantham Journal, Little Gonerby, Spittlegate and Melton Mowbray Advertiser; Grantham Journal, Melton Mowbray, Bourn and Rutland Advertiser.*

Lincoln, Rutland and Stamford Mercury.

Sleaford Gazette and South Lincolnshire Advertiser.

Spalding Free Press and Eastern Counties Advertiser later: *Lincolnshire, Boston and Spalding Free Press and Eastern Counties Advertiser; Lincolnshire, Boston and Spalding Free Press (South Holland and Eastern Counties Advertiser).*

b) **National**

English Labourer.

Labour League Examiner.

Labourer.

Labourers' Union Chronicle later: *National Agricultural Labourers' Chronicle and Industrial Pioneer.*

2. *Official Denominational Publications, including Preaching*

Plans

Lincoln Circuit. The Lord's Day Plan of the Preachers called Primitive Methodists: known also by the name of Ranters (1821) Lincoln Reference Library, Broadsheet 946.

Minutary Records: being Rules, Regulations and Reports made and published by the Primitive Methodist Connexion I, 1814-30 (Leeds, 1854); II, 1831-40 (Leeds, 1852); III, 1841-50 (Leeds, 1852); IV, 1851-5 (Burnley, 1855); V, 1856-60 (Leeds, 1863); VI, 1861-5 (Bradford, 1866) Robert Smith (ed.), [vol. VI, Robert Smythe [sic]].

Minutary Records of the Primitive Methodist Connexion VII, 1866-70; VIII, 1871-5 (Horbury, 1882) J. Ayrton (ed.).

Primitive Methodist Magazine 1-10 (1819-29); n.s. 1 (1830); n.s. 1-12 (1831-42); 1-20, third [sic] ser. (1843-62); n.s. 1-13 (1863-75).

3. *Parliamentary Reports and Papers*

In date order with volume and reference or command numbers.

Numbers 1-4, 6-9, 11-14 and 19-23 relate to population; numbers 5, 16-18 relate to employment conditions; number 10 relates to religion; number 15 to housing; number 24 to friendly societies; number 25 to agriculture.

   1. 1801-2 VII (9) Population, Great Britain. Abstract of Answers and Returns, pursuant to Act 41 Geo. 3 for taking an Account of the Population of Great Britain in 1801.

2. 1812 XI (316) Population Returns of 1811, Abstract of Enumeration Returns 1811.

3. 1822 XV (502) Population of Great Britain, 1821.

4. 1831 XVIII (348) Comparative Account of the Population of Great Britain, in the years 1801, 1811, 1821, and 1831 . . .

5. 1843 XII (510) Reports of the Special Assistant Poor Law Commissioners on the Employment of Women and Children in Agriculture.

6. 1843 XXII (496) Population. Enumeration Abstract, 1841.

7. 1852-3 LXXXV (1631) Population of Great Britain. Population Tables I, Number of Inhabitants in 1801, 1811, 1821, 1831, 1841, 1851.

8. 1852-3 LXXXVI (1632) Population of Great Britain. Population Tables I, Number of Inhabitants in 1801, 1811, 1821, 1831, 1841, 1851, Division VII, North Midland Division.

9. 1852-3 LXXXVIII (1691-II) Population. Ages, Civil Condition, Occupations, &c. Tables II . . .

10. 1852-3 LXXXIX (1690) Population of Great Britain, 1851. Religious Worship (England and Wales).

11. 1862 XVII (2977) Births, Deaths and Marriages (England). Twenty-third Annual Report of the Registrar General for Births, Deaths and Marriages.

12. 1862 L (3056) Population (England and Scotland). Census of England and Wales . . . Numbers and Distribution of the People.

13. 1863 LIII part I (3221) Population (England and Wales). Census of England and Wales, 1861. General Report.

14. 1863 LIII part II (3221) Population (England and Wales). Census of England and Wales 1861 . . . Abstracts of Ages, Civil Condition, Occupations, and Birthplaces of the People, Division IV, Eastern, to Division XI, Welsh . . .

15. 1865 XXVI (3484) Public Health. Seventh Report of the Medical Officer of the Privy Council, with Appendix, 1864.

16. 1867 XVI (3796) Children's Employment Commission (1862), Sixth Report of the Commissioners, with an Appendix.

17. 1867-8 XVII (4068) Agriculture (Employment of Women and Children). First Report of the Commissioners on the Employment of Children, Young Persons, and Women in Agriculture, with Appendix, part I.

18. 1867-8 XVII (4068-I) Agriculture (Employment of Women and Children). Appendix, part II, Evidence from the Assistant Commissioners.

19. 1872 XVII (C.667) Births, Deaths and Marriages (England). Thirty-third Annual Report of the Registrar General for Births, Deaths and Marriages in England (Abstracts for 1870); with a Summary of Marriages, Births and Deaths registered in Ten Years, 1861-70.

20. 1872 LXVI part I (C.676) Census of England and Wales 1871 . . . Area, Houses and Inhabitants, vol. I, Counties.

21. 1872 LXVI part II (C. 676-I) Census of England

and Wales, 1871 . . . Area, Houses, and Inhabitants, vol. II, Registration or Union Counties.

22. 1873 LXXI part I (C.872) Population (England and Wales). Census of England and Wales, 1871 . . . Age, Civil Condition, Occupations and Birth Places of the People, vol. III.

23. 1873 LXXI part II (C.872-I) Population (England and Wales). General Report, vol. IV, Appendix A.

24. 1877 LXXVII (429-I) Report of the Chief Registrar of Friendly Societies for 1876, part II, Appendix P, Friendly Societies.

25. 1881 XVI (C.2778-II) Agricultural Interests, Digest and Appendix to part I of Evidence taken before the Royal Commission on Agriculture; together with reports of the Assistant Commissioners.

4. *Other Contemporary Printed Sources*

Place of publication is London unless otherwise stated. Where chapters from books by a number of contributors or collections of essays or articles have been cited details are given of the publications in which they appear, while full details of the relevant piece of work are given in the footnotes which refer to them.

a) **Books and Pamphlets**

Ambler, R. W. (ed.)
Lincolnshire Returns of the Census of Religious Worship 1851 (Lincoln Record Society, 72, 1979).

Anon. ed.
The Primitive Pulpit, being Original Sermons and Sketches by Various Ministers of the

Primitive Methodist Connexion, 1 (1857).

Antliff, William
*The Life of Hugh Bourne, Founder of the
Primitive Methodist Connexion*, revised by
Colin C. McKechnie (1892).

Brownson, W. J., Gair, J., Mitchell, T. and
Prosser, D.S.
*Heroic men: the death roll of the Primitive
Methodist ministry, being sketches of those
ministers who have died between the
conferences of 1888-9* . . . [1889].

Checkland, S.G. and E.O.A. (eds.)
The Poor Law Report of 1834 (Penguin edn,
Harmondsworth, 1974).

Church, Thomas
Sketches of Primitive Methodism (1847).

*Gospel Victories: or missionary anecdotes of
imprisonments, labours and persecutions
endured by Primitive Methodist preachers
between the years 1812 and 1842* (1851).

Clarke, John Algernon
*Fen Sketches, being a Description of the
Alluvial District known as the Great Level of
the Fens, with a Brief History of its Progressive
Improvements in Drainage and Agriculture*
(1852).

[Clowes, William]
*The Journals of William Clowes, a Primitive
Methodist Preacher . . . from the Year 1810 to
that of 1838* (1844).

Cooper, Thomas
The Life of Thomas Cooper written by

Himself (1877).

[Creasey, James]
Sketches Illustrative of the Topography and History of New and Old Sleaford, in the County of Lincoln, and of Several Places in the Surrounding Neighbourhood (Sleaford, 1825).

Davison, John
The Life of the Venerable William Clowes: one of the founders of the Primitive Methodist Connexion (1854).

[Dow, Lorenzo]
The Dealings of God, Man and the Devil, as Exemplified in the Life, Experience and Travels of Lorenzo Dow (New York, 1850).

Garner, William
The Life of the Rev. and Venerable William Clowes: one of the patriarchs of the Primitive Methodist Connexion (1868).

[Greenwood, Cornelius]
A Short Account of the Late Thomas Fawcett, to which is added the Rise and Progress of Methodism in Sleaford (Sleaford, 1839).

Gutch, Mrs and Peacock, Mabel
Examples of Printed Folk-Lore Concerning Lincolnshire (1908; repr. Liechtenstein, 1967).

Heath, Richard
The English Via Dolorosa or Glimpses of the History of the Agricultural Labourer (1884).

Herod, George
Biographical Studies of Some of Those Preachers whose Labours contributed to the Origination and Early Extension of the

Primitive Methodist Connexion (n.d.).

Jessopp, Augustus
Arcady: for better for worse (1887).

[A Layman]
Memoir of the Life and Labours of Mr. John Wedgwood (1870).

Leigh, Harvey
'Praying Johnny'; or the Life and Labours of John Oxtoby, Primitive Methodist Minister (6th edn, 1867).

Lowe, Thomas (ed.)
Burning Words; or, Choice Remains of the late Rev. Robert Key, of Norfolk (Barnsley, 1882).

Marratt, W.
The History of Lincolnshire: topographical, historical and descriptive, 1 (Boston, 1814).

[Oliver, George]
Scopwickiana; or Sketches and Illustrations of a Secluded Village in Lincolnshire (Lincoln, 1838).

Petty, John
The History of the Primitive Methodist Connexion, from its Origin to the Conference of 1860, the First Jubilee Year of the Connexion, revised and enlarged by James Macpherson (1880).

Sanderson, W. and Harland, W.
Trophies of Grace or the Power of Religion Manifested (Hull, 1839).

Sage, Josiah
The Memoirs of Josiah Sage: concering Joseph

Arch and the pioneering days of trade unionism among the agricultural workers (1951).

Shaw, George
The Life of John Oxtoby, ('Praying Johnny') (Hull, 1894).

Taft, Z.
Biographical Sketches of the Lives and Public Ministry of Various Holy Women . . . vol. 2 (Leeds, 1828).

Walford, John
Memoirs of the Life and Labours of the Late Venerable Hugh Bourne 2 vols (1855-6).

[Walker, George] An Old Fashioned Methodist
Methodist Ritualism, or a Few Thoughts on the Methodism of To-day [1855].

White, William
History, Gazeteer, and Directory of Lincolnshire . . . (1856; repr. Newton Abbot, 1969).

Wrigley, C. J. (ed.)
The Working Classes in the Victorian Age, 4: *rural conditions 1815-1870; debates on the issues from 19th century critical journals* (Farnborough, 1973).

[Young, Arthur]
General View of the Agriculture of the County of Lincoln (2nd edn, 1813; repr. Newton Abbot, 1970).

b) **Periodical Articles**

Anon.
'The Church in Lincolnshire', *Union Review* 3 (1865) 259-75.

[Letter on Ranter Meetings], *Christian Remembrancer* 1 (Aug. 1819) 469-71.

[Letter on the Ranters], *Christian Remembrancer* 3 (Mar. 1821) 136-8.

'The Origin of the Primitive Methodist Connexion', *London Quarterly Review* 67, n.s. 3 (Oct. 1886) 18-40.

Clarke, John Algernon
'Farming of Lincolnshire', *Journal of the Royal Agricultural Society of England* 12 (1851) 258-414.

Pusey, Ph.
'On the Agricultural Improvements of Lincolnshire', *Journal of the Royal Agricultural Society of England* 4 (1843) 287-316.

5. Secondary Sources

See notes under section 4. *Other Contemporary Printed Sources.*

a) **Books and Pamphlets**

Anon.
Heckington in the Eighteen Seventies (Heckington, [1980]).

Lincolnshire Archives Committee, Archivists' Reports 10 (1 Apr. 1958 - 14 Mar. 1959).

Baker, Derek (ed.)
The Church in Town and Countryside: papers read at the seventeenth summer meeting and eighteenth winter meeting of the Ecclesiastical History Society (Oxford, 1979).

Baker, Frank
A Charge to Keep: an introduction to the people called Methodists (1947; repr. 1954).

Beastall, T. W.
The Agricultural Revolution in Lincolnshire (Lincoln, 1978).

Carwardine, Richard
Transatlantic Revivalism: popular evangelicalism in Britain and America 1790-1865 (1978).

Chadwick, Owen
The Victorian Church, 2 parts (1966 and 1970).

Cole, R. E. G.
History of the Manor and Township of Doddington, otherwise Doddington-Pigot in the County of Lincoln . . . (Lincoln, 1897).

Cuming, C. J. and Baker, Derek (eds.)
Popular Belief and Practice: papers read at the ninth summer meeting and tenth winter meeting of the Ecclesiastical History Society (Cambridge, 1972).

Darby, H. C.
The Draining of the Fens (1940; second edn, 1956, repr. Cambridge, 1968).

Dunbabin, J. P. D.
Rural Discontent in Nineteenth-Century Britain (1974).

Ensor, R. C. K.
England 1870-1914 (1936; repr. Oxford, 1960).

Grigg, David
The Agricultural Revolution in South Lincolnshire (Cambridge, 1966).

Harrison, Brian
Drink and the Victorians: the temperance question in England 1815-72 (1971).

Hasbach, W.
A History of the English Agricultural Labourer (1908; repr. 1966).

Hempton, David
Methodism and Politics in British Society 1750-1850 (paperback edn, 1987).

Hobsbawm, E. J.
Primitive Rebels: studies in archaic forms of social movements in the 19th and 20th centuries (1959; repr. Manchester, 1971).

Kendall, H. B.
The Origin and History of the Primitive Methodist Church 2 vols. [*c.* 1905]).

Kent, John
Holding the Fort: studies in Victorian revivalism (1978).

Leary, William
Methodist Preaching Plans: a guide to their usefulness to the historian (Sudbrooke, 1977).

Machin, G. I. T.
Politics and the Churches in Great Britain 1832 to 1868 (Oxford, 1977).

Malcolmson, Robert W.
Popular Recreations in English Society 1700-1850 (Cambridge, 1973).

Mingay, G. E. (ed.)
The Victorian Countryside 2 vols. (1981).

Norman, E. R.
Church and Society in England 1770-1970: a historical study (Oxford, 1976).

Obelkevich, James
Religion and Rural Society: south Lindsey 1825-1875 (Oxford, 1976).

Olney, R. J.
Lincolnshire Politics 1832-1885 (Oxford, 1973).

Rural Society and County Government in Nineteenth-Century Lincolnshire (Lincoln, 1979).

Owen, Dorothy M.
Church and Society in Medieval Lincolnshire (Lincoln, 1971).

Padley, James Saunby
The Fens and Floods of Mid-Lincolnshire; with a Description of the River Witham in its Neglected State before 1762, and its Improvements up to 1825 (Lincoln, 1882).

Pelling, Henry
Politics and Society in Late Victorian Britain (1968).

Perkins, J. A.
Sheep Farming in Eighteenth and Early Nineteenth Century Lincolnshire (Sleaford, 1977).

Pevsner, Nikolaus and Harris, John
The Buildings of England: Lincolnshire
(Harmondsworth, 1964).

Samuel, Raphael (ed.)
Village Life and Labour (1975).

Scotland, Nigel
Methodism and the Revolt of the Field: a study of the Methodist contribution to agricultural trade unionism in East Anglia 1872-96 (Gloucester, 1981).

Sheils, W. J. and Wood, Diana (eds.)
Voluntary Religion: papers read at the 1985 summer meeting and 1986 winter meeting of the Ecclesiastical History Society (Oxford, 1986).

Snell, K. D. M.
Annals of the Labouring Poor: social and agrarian change in England, 1660-1900 (Cambridge, 1985).

Thirsk, Joan
English Peasant Farming: the agrarian history of Lincolnshire from Tudor to recent times (1957).

Townsend, W. J., Workman, H. B. and Eayrs, George (eds.)
A New History of Methodism 2 vols (1909).

Turner, John Munsey
Conflict and Reconciliation: studies in Methodism and Ecumenism in England 1740-1982 (1985).

Valenze, Deborah M.
Prophetic Sons and Daughters: female

preaching and popular religion in industrial England (Princeton, 1985).

Vincent, John
The Formation of the British Liberal Party 1857-1868 (1966; Penguin edn, Harmondsworth, 1972).

Ward, W. R.
Religion and Society in England 1790-1850 (1972).

Wearmouth, Robert F.
Methodism and the Working-Class Movements of England 1800-1850 (1937).

Werner, Julia Stewart
The Primitive Methodist Connexion: its background and early history (Wisconsin, 1984).

Wheeler, W. H.
A History of the Fens of South Lincolnshire: being a description of the Rivers Witham and Welland and their estuary, and an account of the reclamation, drainage, and enclosure of the fens adjacent thereto, 1868; 2nd enlarged edn, Boston, [1896]).

Wilkinson, John T.
Hugh Bourne 1772-1852 (1952).

William Clowes 1780-1851 (1951).

Wright, Neil R.
Lincolnshire Towns and Industry 1700-1914 (Lincoln, 1982).

Wrigley, E. A. and Schofield, R. S.
The Population History of England 1541-1871:

a reconstruction (1981).

b) **Periodical articles**

Ambler, R. W.
'Religious Life in Kesteven - A Return of the Number of Places of Worship not of the Church of England', *Lincolnshire History and Archaeology* 20 (1985) 59-64.

Barley, M. W.
'The Lincolnshire Village and its Buildings', *Lincolnshire Historian* 7 (Spring 1951) 252-72.

Fuller, G. Joan
'Development of Drainage, Agriculture and Settlement in the Fens of South-East Lincs. during the 19th Century', *East Midland Geographer* 1 (June 1957) 3-15.

Grigg, D. B.
'The Land Tax Returns', *Agricultural History Review* 11 (1963) 82-94.

Healey, Kenneth
'"Methodism or Nothing . . ." (in Gedney Marsh, 1856)', *Epworth Witness and Journal of the Lincolnshire Methodist History Society* 2 (Autumn 1975) 133-7.

Holderness, B. A.
'"Open" and "Close" Parishes in England in the Eighteenth and Nineteenth Centuries', *Agricultural History Review* 20 (1972) 126-39.

Mills, Dennis
'English Villages in the Eighteenth and Nineteenth Centuries; a Sociological Approach, part I: the concept of a sociological classification', *Amateur Historian* 6 (Summer

1965) 271-8.

Mills, Dennis R.
'Enclosure in Kesteven', *Agricultural History Review* 7 (1959) 82-97.

Mills, Dennis R.
'Regions of Kesteven devised for Purposes of Agricultural History', *Lincolnshire Architectural and Archaeological Society Reports and Papers*, n.s. 7 (1957) 60-82.

Mills, D. R.
'The Poor Laws and the Distribution of Population *c.* 1600-1860, with special reference to Lincolnshire', *Transactions and Papers of the Institute of British Geographers* 26 (1959) 185-95.

Index

Places are in Lincolnshire unless otherwise indicated

of, 75. *See also*: Christ; God
Lord's Day, the: *see* Sunday
Loughborough Leics., circuit, 31
Louth, 37, 38; area, 38
Luther, Martin, 65

Macclesfield, Ches., 29. *See also*: Independent Methodists
Mackinder, Harwood, 24
Magic Methodists, of Delamere Forest, Ches., 28. *See also*:
    Crawfoot, James
Magistrates, 20
Manchester, Lancs.: *see* Band Room Methodists
Mangles, 19
Manse, furniture fund for, Boston circuit, 69
Manufacturers, 23. *See also*: Lincolnshire, south
Manures, 12
Market places: *see* Bourne, Donington
Market Rasen, 37; area, 38; Wesleyan Methodist circuit, 38
Market towns, 21, 26, 85; and the development of Methodism, 77;
    and the development of trade unionism, 84. *See also*: Boston;
    Bourne; Grantham; Holbeach; lectures; Lincoln;
    Lincolnshire, south, towns; Sleaford; Spalding; Stamford;
    Sutton Bridge; Sutton, Long
Markets, 11
Marriage, 26, 52
Marsh, The, 38
Martin, place of worship at, 56; Primitive Methodist chapel, 56, 57;
Meadow, 13
Meadows, Grace, of Rippingale, 47, 52
Meadows, Sarah of Rippingale, 53
Mechanics: *see* occupations
Meeting houses: *see* chapels
Membership, Methodist, 8; distribution of Primitive Methodist
    membership, 68; Primitive Methodist, effect of agricultural
    trade unionism on, 82; tickets: *see* classes. *See also*: Boston;
    Donington; Gosberton Clough; Holbeach; Holbeach Bank;
    Kyme, South; Lincoln; Little London; Primitive Methodists;
    Spalding; Whaplode Drove
Messingham: *see* Sharp, Samuel